SIMP ....   JUS FOOD FC

Also by the author:
Simply Delicious
A Simply Delicious Christmas
Simply Delicious 2
Simply Delicious Fish
Simply Delicious in France & Italy
Simply Delicious Versatile Vegetables
Simply Delicious Meals in Minutes
Darina Allen's Simply Delicious Recipes
Irish Traditional Cooking

Darina Allen

SIMPLY

DELICIOUS

Food for Family &

Friends

Gill and Macmillan
and
Radio Telefís Éireann

Published by
Gill and Macmillan Ltd
Goldenbridge
Dublin 8
and
Radio Telefís Éireann
Donnybrook
Dublin 4
www.gillmacmillan.ie
© Darina Allen 1993
0 7171 2060 0
Photographs by RTE/Des Gaffney
Food styling by Rory O'Connell
Typeset by
Seton Music Graphics Ltd, Bantry, Co. Cork
Colour origination by
D.O.T.S., Dublin
Printed by
ColourBooks Ltd, Dublin

A catalogue record is available for this book
from the British Library

12   14   16   15   13

I dedicate this book to my mother, Elizabeth O'Connell, whose food has nourished and comforted me throughout the years.

Contents

FOREWORD   xi

ACKNOWLEDGMENTS   xiii

GLOSSARY   xv

SOUPS
  ^v Tomato and Basil Soup   1
  ^v Tomato and Mint Soup   2
  ^v Potato and Parsley Soup   3
  Winter Vegetable Soup   4
  French Peasant Soup   4
  Chicken Stock   5
  ^v Vegetable Stock   7

MEAT   8
  * Roast Rib of Beef with Horseradish Sauce, Gravy and
    Yorkshire Pudding   9
  ^v Yorkshire Pudding with Olives   12
  ^v Mustard and Thyme Yorkshire Pudding   12
  Steak with Irish Whiskey and Tarragon   12
  * Scalloped Potato with Steak and Kidney   13
  Stir-fried Beef with Oyster Sauce   14
  * Basic Hamburgers   15
  * Hamburgers with Mushroom à la Crème and Crispy Bacon 16
  * Hamburgers with Guacamole and French Fried Onions   17
  * Hamburgers with Blue Cheese, Sweet Cucumber Salad and
    Tomato Relish   18
  Roast Loin of Lamb with Duxelle Stuffing and Mint Sauce 19
  Lamb Chops Duxelle   21
  Epigrams   21
  Lamb Chops with Mint and Butter Sauce   21
  Lamb Stew with Bacon, Onions and Garden Herbs   22
  * Mild Madras Curry with Fresh Spices, with Cucumber and
    Yoghurt Raita and Hot Chilli Sauce   23
  * Roast Stuffed Fillet of Pork with Apple Sauce   26
  Carbonnade of Pork   28

Homemade Sausages with Apple Sauce 29
Traditional Roast Stuffed Chicken with Parsley Sauce 30
Chicken Cordon Bleu 32
* Shanagarry Chicken or Pheasant Casserole 33
* Shanagarry Chicken Casserole with Herb Crust 34
Spiced Chicken with Almonds 35

FISH 36
Pangrilled Fish with Parsley Butter and Tomato Fondue 36
Cod with Mushrooms and Buttered Crumbs 37
Scallop Shell of Seafood 39

EGGS, CHEESE AND PANCAKES 41
ᵛ * French Omelette 41
ᵛ Macaroni Cheese 42
ᵛ Cheddar Cheese Soufflé with Chives 43
ᵛ * Irish Cheddar Cheese Croquettes 44
* Pancakes 46
ᵛ * Savoury Pancake Batter 46
ᵛ * Herb Pancakes 46
ᵛ * Almspurses with Tomato Sauce 47
* Seafood Pancakes 48
* Chicken, Ham and Spring Onion Pancakes 49
* Stuffed Pancakes, Pancake Parcels and variations 49

VEGETARIAN DISHES 51
ᵛ * A Warm Salad of Irish Goat's Cheese with Walnut Oil
Dressing 51
ᵛ ᵛᵛ* Black-eyed Beans with Mushrooms 52
ᵛ ᵛᵛ Chick Peas with Fresh Spices 54
ᵛ ᵛᵛ Pasta 54
ᵛ ᵛᵛ Spaghetti with Fresh Tomato Sauce 55
ᵛ ᵛᵛ Pasta Olé, Olé, Olé 55
ᵛ ᵛᵛ Spaghetti with Olive Oil and Garlic 56
ᵛ ᵛᵛ* Stir-fried Vegetables 56

VEGETABLES 58
ᵛ * Gratin of Potato and Spring Onion 59
ᵛ * Gratin of Potato and Mushrooms 60
* Gratin of Potato and Smoked Salmon 60
ᵛ * Baked Potatoes 61
ᵛ ᵛᵛ* Rustic Roast Potatoes 62
ᵛ ᵛᵛ Crusty Potatoes with Ginger and Garlic 62

^v * Potato Cakes — 63
^{v vv}* The Perfect Chip — 64
^{v vv} Straw Potatoes — 64
^{v vv} Matchstick Potatoes — 64
^{v vv} Mignonette Potatoes — 64
^{v vv} Pont Neuf Potatoes — 64
^{v vv} Jumbo Chips — 64
^{v vv} Buffalo Chips — 64
^{v vv} Potato Crisps or Game Chips — 65
^{v vv} Garlic Crisps — 65
^v * Potato Salad — 65
^{v vv}* Roast Onions — 66
^{v vv}* Roast Parsnips — 66
^v Glazed Carrots — 66
^v Cauliflower Cheese — 67
^v Leeks Mornay — 68
Ham and Leek Mornay — 68
^{v vv} Tomato Fondue — 68
^{v vv} Piperonata — 69
^{v vv} Kinoith Summer Garden Salad — 70

PUDDINGS — 71
^v Chocolate Fudge Pudding — 71
^v * Bread and Butter Pudding — 72
^v * Cullohill Apple Pie — 73
^v Cullohill Rhubarb Tart — 74
^v Dutch Apple Cake — 74
^v Apple Crumble — 75
^v Blackberry and Apple Crumble — 76
^v Rhubarb Crumble — 76
^v Rhubarb and Strawberry Crumble — 76
^v Gooseberry Crumble — 76
^v Gooseberry and Elderflower Crumble — 76
^v Plum or Apricot Crumble — 76
^v * Caramelised Honey and Almond Tart — 76
^v * John Desmond's Crêpe Soufflée — 77
^v * Crêpes with Orange Butter — 79
^{v vv}* Strawberry and Rhubarb Compote — 80
^v Rhubarb Fool — 81
^v Green Gooseberry Fool — 81
^v Green Gooseberry and Elderflower Fool — 82
^{v vv} A Fresh Fruit Salad — 82
^v Hazel's Bananas in Cointreau — 83

^v Light Vanilla Ice Cream with Chocolate, Butterscotch,
    Fresh Raspberry, Blackcurrant or Apricot Sauce   83–85
^v Almond Meringue with Strawberries and Cream   85
^v American Popovers   86

IRISH FARMHOUSE CHEESES   87

BREADS, BISCUITS AND CAKES   91
^v * White Soda Bread and Scones   91
^v * White Soda Bread with Herbs   92
^v * Maria Moloney's Herb and Cheese Scones   92
^v * Spotted Dog   93
^v * Timmy's Deep Pan Pizza   93
^v * Individual Soda Bread Pizzas   94
^v * Simply Nutritious Wholemeal Bread   94
^v Banana Bread   95
^v * Florence Bowe's Crumpets   96
^v Oatmeal Biscuits   97
^v Florrie's Chocolate and Toffee Squares   98
^v Pearl McGillicuddy's All-in-One Buns   99
^v Butterfly Buns   99
^v Chocolate Sandwich   100
^v Coffee Cake   101
^v Julia Wight's Carrot Cake   102

JAMS   104
^{v vv} Seville Marmalade made with Whole Oranges   104
^{v vv} Strawberry Jam   105
^{v vv} Mrs Mackey's Uncooked Strawberry or Raspberry Jam   106
^{v vv} Crab Apple or Bramley Apple Jelly   106
^{v vv} Sweet Geranium Jelly   107
^{v vv} Clove Jelly   107
^{v vv} Mint Jelly   107
^{v vv} Rosemary Jelly   107

STORE CUPBOARD STANDBYS   108

* recipes demonstrated on RTE's *Simply Delicious Food for Family &*
Friends television series
^v recipes suitable for non-vegan vegetarians
^{vv} recipes suitable for vegans

Foreword

This book is not about fancy entertaining; it's about sharing delicious, wholesome, comforting food with family and friends around the kitchen table. All of my happiest childhood memories are tied up with food — the smell of crusty bread baking in the oven or maybe a stew bubbling on the side of the stove. For me the most important food is that which warms and nourishes and brings the family together.

One of the greatest reassurances any of us can have, particularly as children and teenagers, is the knowledge that when we arrive home tired and weary, someone will be there with a meal ready to revive us. The people who provide these endless meals are precious beyond words, and are mostly taken totally for granted. Remember always to murmur thank-you before you rush out again, and a little hug every now and then works wonders, because for many people cooking can be a never-ending and thankless task.

Those of you who have taken the time to read the forewords to my other books will know that I am passionate about the idea of families sitting down together at least once a day — not always easy as the American 'grab, gobble and go' culture threatens to engulf us, even over here. Nonetheless it is well worth making the effort to lay a pretty, welcoming table. Then the food, no matter how simple, is all the more likely to taste delicious!

There are many people who don't altogether enjoy cooking for various reasons — perhaps because they are struggling with an impossibly low budget or are constantly pressed for time. For them the endless drudgery of preparing daily meals is a penance which they deeply resent, and alas that resentment quickly shows in the final result. To these disenchanted cooks, let me say just one thing: the satisfaction to be derived from taking a freshly baked loaf out of the oven or making a delectable soup is positively tangible. Sadly, there is no buzz to be had at all from slicing open a packet — and some people even feel slight guilt pangs which they scarcely admit to themselves. I really hope this book will help all cooks to discover that providing delicious homemade food for the family needn't necessarily take a long time — and can be a thoroughly enjoyable process.

A weekly plan of action can be an enormous help, particularly if you are working as well as looking after the family. Sit down for a few minutes on Sunday, put your feet up and loosely plan your weekly menu, remembering what is in season. As far as possible avoid expensive convenience food and use fresh, naturally produced ingredients that will nourish your family and safeguard their health.

Besides buying fresh produce, it is also worth trying to discover as far as possible where and how the food in your local shops is being produced. We should all encourage our shops and supermarkets to identify their sources and to sell meat, and particularly vegetables, marked with the producer's name. This means the good producer will get credit for extra effort, and the consumer, having discovered good produce, will easily be able to find it again.

My choice of recipes for this book was obviously influenced by the food my own family enjoy. At first glance you may think that some of the recipes, such as apple pie or chicken casserole, sound a bit old hat, but I make no apology for including these old favourites. They are classics which have stood the test of time, and over the years I have worked on the recipes to produce what I hope is an especially delicious version.

As few people nowadays can spend hours in the kitchen sweating over the stove, I've included a large number of very fast recipes, and many of my 'great convertibles' — endlessly adaptable recipes which form the backbone of family cooking. There is also a section on vegetarian cooking, something which excites me and is particularly relevant now that the number of vegetarians is increasing so dramatically.

I hope that you, your family and friends will enjoy sharing some of this food around the kitchen table, for that, after all, is what life is all about. Happy cooking!

Darina Allen

Shanagarry, Co. Cork

November 1992

Acknowledgments

Seven books down the road, I realise that the army of helpers on whom I rely has grown to such an extent that it would take another whole book to thank them all adequately! In the preparation of *Simply Delicious Food for Family & Friends* I am grateful in particular to my loyal and valiant staff at the Ballymaloe Cookery School: Claire Wenham, Breda Murphy and Rachel O'Neill who tested and retested the recipes, and my secretaries Rosalie Dunne and Adrienne Morrissey who typed and retyped the manuscript.

I also owe a special word of thanks to the dedicated food producers we visited while filming the television series which this book accompanies: Sean Loughnane, the innovative and charismatic butcher from Galway who finishes the animals on his own farm to ensure top quality antibiotic- and hormone-free meat; Pat McCarthy, one of a new breed of pig farmers who realises the value of natural production and whose happy pigs we filmed overlooking Inchydoney Strand in West Cork; Robert Putz who breeds sleek and contented Aberdeen Angus on the Durrus Peninsula in West Cork; beekeeper Kevin Walker whose honey we enjoyed at Kilglass, Co. Roscommon; Howard Mills of Crookstown, Co. Cork whose nutty stoneground flour we use for our Irish soda bread.

We also filmed some of the outstanding Irish farmhouse cheesemakers who have made such an important contribution to the Irish food scene in recent years: Giana and Tom Ferguson who make Gubbeen on their farm at Schull in West Cork; Meg and Derrick Gordon who make St Tola and Lough Caum cheese from goat's milk at Inagh, Co. Clare; Jane and Louis Grubb who make Cashel Blue and Cashel White at Fethard, Co. Tipperary; Veronica and Norman Steele who make Milleens on the Beara Peninsula. All these dedicated food producers and many others like them give me hope for the future.

I also want to thank John Desmond, who made us the ultimate pancake in his restaurant on Hare Island off the West Cork coast; Luke Dodd, the effervescent young curator of Strokestown House, Co. Roscommon, which provided a wonderful backdrop to the programme on spices; and Nimmo's Restaurant near the Spanish Arch in Galway who let us film at just a moment's notice.

Once again, Des Gaffney and Denis O'Farrell deserve honourable mention for their inspired food photographs, styled as usual by my wonderfully artistic brother Rory O'Connell.

I am grateful as ever to my producer and director Colette Farmer and the hardworking RTE team who followed me round the country and into the kitchen with great good humour and patience: Roy Bedell, Kevin Cummins, John Rogers, Gary Finnegan, Harry Heuston and Joe Kerins.

Last but far from least, I want to thank my parents-in-law Ivan and Myrtle Allen who continue to encourage and inspire me, and of course my dear husband Tim who cooks our family supper so that I can write books.

Glossary

Bain marie (or water bath): Can be any deep container, half-filled with hot water, in which delicate foods, e.g. custards or fish mousses, are cooked in their moulds or terrines. The bain marie is put into a low or moderate oven and the food is protected from direct heat by the gentle, steamy atmosphere, without risk of curdling. The term bain marie is also used for a similar container which holds several pans to keep soups, vegetables or stews warm during restaurant service.

Blanch: This cooking term can be confusing because it's used in many different senses. Usually it means to immerse food in water and to bring to the boil, parcook, extract salt or to loosen skins as in the case of almonds.

Deglaze: After meat has been sautéed or roasted, the pan or roasting dish is degreased and then a liquid is poured into the pan to dissolve the coagulated and caramelised pan juices. This is the basis of many sauces and gravies. The liquid could be water, stock or alcohol, e.g. wine or brandy.

Degrease: To remove surplus fat from a liquid or a pan, either by pouring off or by skimming the surface with a spoon.

Egg wash: A raw egg beaten with a pinch of salt, it is brushed on raw tarts, pies, buns and biscuits to give them a shiny, golden glaze when cooked.

Roux: Equal quantities of butter and flour cooked together for 2 minutes over a gentle heat. This mixture may be whisked into boiling liquid to thicken, e.g. gravies, sauces, milk etc. It can be kept in the fridge and used when needed. (See Shanagarry Chicken Casserole, p. 33.)

Unsweetened chocolate: Is just that — chocolate which does not contain any sugar. If it is unobtainable use ordinary chocolate but adjust the amount of sugar accordingly or substitute 3 tablespoons of unsweetened cocoa and $\frac{1}{2}$ oz (15 g) unsalted butter for every 1 oz (30 g) unsweetened chocolate.

Measurements
All imperial spoon measurements in this book are rounded measurements unless the recipe states otherwise. All American spoon measurements are level.

Temperature Conversion
Approximate fahrenheit/centigrade equivalents are given in the recipes, but for fan or convection ovens it is wise to check the manufacturer's instructions regarding temperature conversion.

Soups

A really smashing soup based on homemade stock with lots of bits in it is a terrific standby — appetising, warming, nourishing and of course marvellously filling. With some fresh, crusty bread it is virtually a meal in itself. I always have three or four different soups in the freezer. I put them in plastic milk cartons, and if I'm stuck for time I cut the carton off the soup while it is still frozen. It can be defrosted in a microwave in a few minutes, but I have often resorted to putting a whole frozen block of soup in a saucepan and you would be surprised at how quickly it thaws and reheats! It is also well worth freezing individual portions so that children can help themselves.

ᵛ*Tomato and Basil Soup*

Serves 5

We worked for a long time to try and make this soup reasonably fool-proof. Good quality tinned tomatoes (a must for your store cupboard) give a really good result. Homemade tomato purée although delicious can give a more variable result depending on the quality of the tomatoes.

> $1\frac{1}{4}$ pints (750 ml/3 cups) homemade tomato purée (see below)
>   *or* 2 x 14 oz (400 g) tins of tomatoes, liquidised and sieved
> 1 small onion, finely chopped
> $\frac{1}{2}$ oz (15 g/$\frac{1}{8}$ stick) butter
> 8 fl ozs (250 ml/1 cup) Béchamel sauce (white) (see below)
> 8 fl ozs (250 ml/1 cup) homemade chicken stock *or* vegetable stock
>   (see pp 5–7)
> 2 tablesp. (2 American tablesp. + 2 teasp.) freshly chopped basil
> salt, freshly ground pepper and sugar
> 4 fl ozs (120 ml/$\frac{1}{2}$ cup) cream
>
> *Garnish*
> whipped cream
> fresh basil leaves

Sweat the onion in the butter on a gentle heat until soft but not coloured. Add the tomato purée (or chopped tinned tomatoes plus juice), white sauce and homemade chicken stock. Add the chopped basil, season with salt, freshly ground pepper and sugar. Bring to the boil and simmer for a few minutes.

Liquidise, taste and dilute further if necessary. Bring back to the boil, correct seasoning and serve with the addition of a little cream if necessary. Garnish with a tiny blob of whipped cream and some basil.

Note: This soup needs to be tasted carefully as the final result depends on the quality of the tomato purée, stock etc.

ᵛ*Tomato and Mint Soup*
Substitute Spearmint or Bowles mint for basil in the recipe above.

ᵛ*Béchamel Sauce*

> $\frac{1}{2}$ pint (300 ml/1$\frac{1}{4}$ cups) milk
> few slices of carrot
> few slices of onion
> 3 peppercorns
> small sprig of thyme
> small sprig of parsley
> 1$\frac{1}{2}$ ozs (45 g/scant $\frac{1}{3}$ cup) roux (see p. 34 *or* glossary)
> salt and freshly ground pepper

This is a wonderfully quick way of making Béchamel Sauce if you have roux already made. Put the cold milk into a saucepan with the carrot, onion, peppercorns, thyme and parsley. Bring to the boil, simmer for 4–5 minutes, remove from the heat and leave to infuse for 10 minutes. Strain out the vegetables, bring the milk back to the boil and thicken to a light coating consistency by whisking in roux. Season with salt and freshly ground pepper, taste and correct the seasoning if necessary.

ᵛ ᵛᵛ*Tomato Purée*
Tomato purée is one of the very best ways of preserving the flavour of ripe summer tomatoes for winter use. We make large quantities of this purée at the end of summer when tomatoes are inexpensive and we find it indispensable for soups, stews and casseroles in winter.

> 2 lbs (900 g) very ripe tomatoes
> 1 small onion, chopped
> good pinch of salt
> few twists of black pepper
> 2 teasp. sugar

Cut the tomatoes into quarters and put into a stainless steel saucepan with the onion, salt, freshly ground pepper and sugar. Cook on a gentle heat until the tomatoes are soft (no water is needed). Put through the fine blade of the mouli-légume or a nylon sieve.

Allow to get cold and refrigerate or freeze.

^v *Potato and Parsley Soup*

Serves 6

Potato soup was my children's absolute favourite when they were little — they couldn't be persuaded to try anything else! They have since become more adventurous but still love it. Most people would have potatoes and onions in the house even if their cupboards were otherwise bare, so one could make this 'simply delicious' soup at a moment's notice. While the vegetables are sweating, pop a few white soda scones into the oven and you will have a nourishing meal.

> **15 ozs (425 g/3 cups) peeled, diced 'old' potatoes — Kerr's Pinks, Golden Wonders, Sharpes Express *or* Pink Fir Apple**
> **2 ozs (55 g/$\frac{1}{2}$ stick) butter**
> **4 ozs (110 g/1 cup) diced onions**
> **1 teasp. (1 American teasp.) salt**
> **freshly ground pepper**
> **5 *or* 6 parsley stalks**
> **1$\frac{1}{2}$ pints (900 ml/3$\frac{3}{4}$ cups) homemade chicken stock *or* vegetable stock (see pp 5–7)**
> **4 fl ozs (130 ml/$\frac{1}{2}$ cup) creamy milk (I use 2 fl ozs (50 ml/$\frac{1}{4}$ cup) each milk and cream)**

> *Garnish*
> **1 tablesp. (1 American tablesp. + 1 teasp.) freshly chopped parsley**

Melt the butter in a heavy saucepan. When it foams, add the potatoes and onions and toss them in the butter until well coated. Sprinkle with salt and freshly ground pepper. Cover and sweat on a gentle heat for 10 minutes. Add the parsley stalks and stock and cook until the vegetables are soft. Remove the stalks and purée the soup in a blender or food processor. Taste and adjust the seasoning. Thin with creamy milk to the required consistency. Serve sprinkled with freshly chopped parsley.

Winter Vegetable Soup

Serves 8–9

We make huge pots of this in winter and I usually keep some in the freezer. Kabanossi, a thin sausage which is now widely available, gives a gutsy, slightly smoky flavour to the soup. Although satisfying, it is by no means essential.

8 ozs (225 g/2 cups) onions, chopped
$10\frac{1}{2}$ ozs (300 g/2 cups) carrots, cut into $\frac{1}{4}$ inch (5 mm) dice
$7\frac{1}{2}$ ozs (215 g/2 cups) celery, cut into $\frac{1}{4}$ inch (5 mm) dice
$4\frac{1}{2}$ ozs (125 g/1 cup) parsnips, cut into $\frac{1}{4}$ inch (5 mm) dice
7 ozs (200 g/1 cup) white part of 2 leeks, cut into $\frac{1}{4}$ inch (5 mm) slices
8 ozs (225 g) rindless streaky bacon, cut into $\frac{1}{4}$ inch (5 mm) lardons
2 tablesp. (2 American tablesp. + 2 teasp.) olive oil
1 Kabanossi sausage*, cut into $\frac{1}{8}$ inch (3 mm) thin slices (optional)
1 x 14 oz (400 g) tin of tomatoes
salt, freshly ground pepper and sugar
3 pints (1.7 L/$7\frac{1}{2}$ cups) homemade chicken stock (see opposite)

Garnish
2 tablesp. (2 American tablesp. + 2 teasp.) freshly chopped parsley

Blanch the chunky bacon lardons, refresh and dry well. Prepare the vegetables. Put the olive oil in a saucepan, add the bacon and sauté over a medium heat until it becomes crisp and golden. Add the chopped onions, carrots and celery, cover and sweat for 5 minutes. Next add the parsnips and finely sliced leeks, cover and sweat for a further 5 minutes. Slice the Kabanossi sausage thinly and add. Chop the tomatoes and add to the rest of the vegetables. Season with salt, freshly ground pepper and sugar. Add the chicken stock. Allow to cook until all the vegetables are tender, 20 minutes approx. Taste and correct the seasoning. Sprinkle with chopped parsley and serve with lots of crusty brown bread.

*If you have difficulty finding Kabanossi sausages, contact Horgan's Delicatessen, Mitchelstown, Co. Cork, tel. (025) 24977. It can be sent by post and will keep for months in the fridge.

French Peasant Soup

Serves 6

This is another very substantial soup: it has 'eating and drinking' in it and would certainly be a meal in itself, particularly with grated Cheddar cheese scattered over the top.

6 ozs (170 g) unsmoked streaky bacon (in the piece)

5 ozs (140 g/1 cup) potatoes, peeled and cut into $\frac{1}{4}$ inch (5 mm) dice

2 ozs (55 g/$\frac{1}{2}$ cup) onions, finely chopped

1 small clove of garlic (optional)

1 lb (450 g) very ripe tomatoes, peeled and diced *or* 1 x 14 oz (400 g)
   tin of tomatoes and their juice

olive *or* sunflower oil

salt and freshly ground pepper

$\frac{1}{2}$–1 teasp. sugar

1$\frac{1}{4}$ pints (750 ml/3 cups) homemade chicken stock (see below)

2 ozs (55 g) cabbage (Savoy is best), finely chopped

Garnish
freshly chopped parsley

Remove the rind from the bacon if necessary. Prepare the vegetables and cut the bacon into $\frac{1}{4}$ inch (5 mm) approx. dice. Blanch the bacon cubes in cold water to remove some of the salt, drain and dry on kitchen paper. Sauté in a little olive or sunflower oil until the fat runs and the bacon is crisp and golden. Add the potatoes, onions and crushed garlic, sweat for 10 minutes and then add the diced tomatoes and any juice. Season with salt, pepper and sugar. Cover with stock and cook for 5 minutes. Add the finely chopped cabbage and continue to simmer just until the cabbage is cooked. Taste and adjust the seasoning. Sprinkle with lots of freshly chopped parsley and serve.

Chicken Stock

Homemade chicken stock is wonderfully useful to have in your fridge or freezer. *Fond* is the French name for stock: *fond* means foundation, which sums up stock perfectly: stocks are the foundation of so many things — soups, sauces, casseroles etc. Making stock is really just an attitude of mind; instead of absent-mindedly flinging things into the bin, keep your carcases, giblets and vegetable trimmings and use them for your stock pot. Nowadays some supermarkets and poulterers are happy to give you chicken carcases and giblets as well, often just for the asking, because there is so little demand.

2–3 raw *or* cooked chicken carcases *or* a mixture of both *or* 1 x 4 lb
   (1.8 kg) boiling fowl, disjointed
giblets from the chicken, i.e. neck, heart, gizzard
6 pints (3.4 L/15 cups) approx. cold water
1 sliced onion

1 leek, split in two
1 stick of celery *or* 1 lovage leaf
1 sliced carrot
few parsley stalks
sprig of thyme
6 peppercorns

Chop up the carcases as much as possible. Put all the ingredients into a saucepan and cover with cold water. Bring to the boil and skim the fat off the top with a tablespoon. Simmer for 3–5 hours. Strain and remove any remaining fat. If you need a stronger flavour, boil down the liquid in an open pan to reduce by one-third or one-half the volume. Do not add salt.

Note: Stock will keep several days in the fridge. If you want to keep it for longer, boil it up again for 5–6 minutes every couple of days; allow it to get cold and refrigerate again. Stock also freezes perfectly. For cheap containers use large yoghurt cartons or plastic milk bottles, then you can cut them off the frozen stock without a conscience if you need to defrost it in a hurry!

In restaurants the stock is usually allowed to simmer uncovered so it will be as clear as possible, but I advise people making stock at home to cover the pot, otherwise the whole house will smell of stock and that may put you off making it on a regular basis.

The above recipe is just a guideline. If you have only one carcase and can't be bothered to make a small quantity of stock, why not freeze the carcase and save it up until you have 6 or 7 carcases plus giblets? Then you can make a really good sized pot of stock and get best value for your fuel.

Chicken liver shouldn't go into the stock pot because it will cause a bitterness in the stock, but the livers make a wonderful smooth pâté which can be served in lots of different ways.

There are some vegetables which should not be put in the stock: potatoes because they soak up flavour and make the stock cloudy; parsnips — too strong; beetroot — too strong also and the dye would produce a red stock! Cabbage or other brassicas give an off-taste on long cooking. A little white turnip is sometimes an asset, but it is very easy to overdo it. I also ban bay leaf in my chicken stocks because I find that the flavour of bay can predominate easily and add a 'sameness' to soups made from the stock later on.

Salt is another ingredient that you will find in most stock recipes, but not in mine. The reason I don't put it in is because if I want to reduce the stock later to make a sauce, it very soon becomes oversalted.

^v*Vegetable Stock*

This is just a rough guide. Basically you can make a vegetable stock from whatever vegetables you have available but try not to use too much of any one vegetable unless you particularly want that flavour to predominate.

> 1 small white turnip
> 2 onions, peeled and roughly sliced *or* the green parts of 2–3 leeks
> 3 sticks of celery, washed and roughly chopped
> 3 large carrots, scrubbed and roughly chopped
> $\frac{1}{2}$ fennel bulb, roughly chopped
> 2 medium-sized potatoes, scrubbed and roughly chopped
> 4–6 parsley stalks
> bouquet garni
> $\frac{1}{4}$ lb (110 g) mushrooms
> few peppercorns
> 4 pints (2.5 L/10 cups) cold water

Put all the ingredients into a large saucepan and add the water. Bring to the boil, then turn the heat down, cover and leave to simmer for $1\frac{1}{2}$–2 hours. Strain through a sieve.

This keeps for a week in the fridge.

Meat

That tempting aroma of roasting meat wafting from the oven is still one of the best ways I know of getting the family into the kitchen at dinner time. We are fortunate in Ireland to have access to superb meat and poultry whose quality is recognised internationally. The picture is not entirely rosy, however. Whether the industry is prepared to admit it or not, it is quite clear to me that Irish meat now has a serious credibility problem. With regular scandals about listeria, salmonella, BSE, angel dust, hormones and antibiotics it is hardly surprising that consumers are confused and wary. The intensive rearing of animals and poultry in conditions which many consider to be inhumane, and the resulting loss of flavour, are also matters of concern to more and more people.

The figures speak for themselves: meat consumption in Ireland has dropped considerably in the last few years. Anxiety about cholesterol has played some part in this, but I am convinced that the other factors are also significant. Teenagers in particular are becoming vegetarian in numbers that cannot be discounted — and I must say that if I had no choice but to eat battery-produced chicken or intensively produced pork, I would become a vegetarian pretty quickly myself.

The meat trade must listen to what people are saying. They must increase their effort to ensure the total elimination of harmful hormones, antibiotics and additives of all kinds, and at the same time actively encourage humane rearing methods. I certainly have no difficulty eating meat when the animals are reared naturally in the open air as they ought to be.

We, as consumers, will have to face the fact that pure meat produced to these methods is bound to cost more; but we should at least be offered the choice between the more highly priced, quality produce of a small-scale farmer and cheaper, mass-produced meat.

Fortunately there is already a discernible trend back to small-scale production in Ireland. The Pure Meat Company in Wexford is just one of a number of enterprises dedicated to promoting naturally produced meat from animals humanely reared on lush grass — and all credit is due to them.

I would like to see butchers everywhere revealing the sources of the meat they sell, so that we can familiarise ourselves with the good producers, and give them the recognition and support they deserve. I would also like to see butchers encouraging farmers to concentrate once again on rearing traditional breeds such as Aberdeen Angus and Shorthorn, which produce such wonderful beef.

One last thing about meat: it really is important to store it correctly. Take it out of its plastic bag as soon as you bring it home, put it on a plate, cover it loosely and put it in the fridge. The larger the joint, the longer it needs to hang. Smaller joints like chops or steaks should be used, if possible, on the day they are bought; otherwise they pick up flavours from the fridge and begin to deteriorate. Mince *must* be used straight away because it turns sour very quickly.

* Roast Rib of Beef with Horseradish Sauce, Gravy and Yorkshire Pudding

Few people can resist a roast rib of beef with horseradish sauce, Yorkshire pudding, lots of gravy and crusty roast potatoes. Always buy beef on the bone for roasting. It will have much more flavour and it isn't difficult to carve.

wing rib of beef on the bone (well-hung)
salt and freshly ground pepper

Gravy

Serves 8–10

1 pint (600 ml/2 $\frac{1}{2}$ cups) stock (preferably homemade beef stock)
roux (optional — see p. 34 *or* glossary)

Ask your butcher to saw through the upper chine bone so that the 'feather bones' will be easy to remove before carving. Weigh the joint and calculate the cooking time (see below).

Preheat the oven to 240°C/475°F/regulo 9.

Score the fat and season with salt and freshly ground pepper. Place the meat in a roasting tin with the fat side uppermost. As the fat renders down in the heat of the oven, it will baste the meat. The bones provide a natural rack to hold the meat clear of the fat in the roasting pan. Put the meat into a fully preheated oven; after 15 minutes turn down the heat to moderate, 180°C/350°F/regulo 4, until the meat is cooked to your taste.

There are various ways of checking. I usually put a skewer into the thickest part of the joint, leave it there for about 30–45 seconds and then

9

put it against the back of my hand. If it still feels cool, the meat is rare; if it is warm, it is medium rare; if it is hotter, it's medium; and if you can't keep the skewer against your hand for more than a second, then you can bet it's well done. Also if you check the colour of the juices you will find they are clear as opposed to red or pink for rare or medium.

If you own a meat thermometer that will eliminate guesswork altogether but make sure the thermometer is not touching a bone when you are testing.

Beef is rare at an internal temperature of   60°C/140°F
      medium at an internal temperature of   70°C/155°F
      well-done at an internal temperature of 75°C/165°F

When the meat is cooked it should be allowed to rest on a plate in a warm oven for 15–30 minutes before carving, depending on the size of the roast. The internal temperature will continue to rise by as much as 2–3°C/5°F, so remove the roast from the oven while it is still slightly underdone.

Meanwhile make the gravy. Spoon the fat off the roasting tin. Pour the stock into the cooking juices remaining in the tin. Boil for a few minutes, stirring and scraping the pan well to dissolve the caramelised meat juices (I find a small whisk ideal for this). Thicken very slightly with a little roux if you like. Taste and add salt and freshly ground pepper if necessary. Strain and serve in a warm gravy boat.

Carve the beef at the table and serve with horseradish sauce, Yorkshire pudding, gravy and lots of crusty roast potatoes.

Roasting times
Since ovens vary enormously in efficiency, some thermostats are not always accurate and some joints of meat are much thicker than others, these figures must be treated as guidelines rather than rules. The times below include the 15 minute searing time at a high heat.

Beef on the bone
Rare   10–12 minutes per 1 lb (450 g)
Medium   12–15 minutes per 1 lb (450 g)
Well-done 18–20 minutes per 1 lb (450 g)

Beef off the bone
Rare   8–10 minutes per 1 lb (450 g)
Medium   10–12 minutes per 1 lb (450 g)
Well-done 15–18 minutes per 1 lb (450 g)

^v*Horseradish Sauce*

Serves 8–10

Horseradish grows wild in many parts of Ireland and looks like giant dock leaves. If you can't find it near you, plant some in your garden. It is very prolific and the root which you grate can be dug up at any time of the year.

$1\frac{1}{2}$ –2 tablesp. (2–2$\frac{1}{2}$ American tablesp.) grated horseradish
2 teasp. wine vinegar
1 teasp. lemon juice
$\frac{1}{4}$ teasp. mustard
$\frac{1}{4}$ teasp. salt
pinch of freshly ground pepper
1 teasp. sugar
8 fl ozs (250 ml/1 cup) softly whipped cream

Scrub the horseradish root well, peel and grate. Put the grated horseradish into a bowl with the wine vinegar, lemon juice, mustard, salt, freshly ground pepper and sugar. Fold in the softly whipped cream but do not over-mix or the sauce will curdle. It keeps for 2–3 days; cover so that it doesn't pick up flavours in the fridge.

This is a fairly mild horseradish sauce. If you want to really 'clear the sinuses', increase the amount of horseradish!

^v*Yorkshire Pudding*

Serves 8–10

Simply irresistible with lots of gravy! I cook individual ones which I'm sure would be very much frowned on in Yorkshire, but if you want to be more traditional cook one large pudding in a roasting tin and cut it into squares.

4 ozs (110 g/scant 1 cup) white flour, preferably unbleached
2 eggs, preferably free-range
$\frac{1}{2}$ pint (300 ml/1$\frac{1}{4}$ cups) milk
$\frac{1}{2}$oz (15 g/$\frac{1}{8}$ stick) butter, melted oil *or* pure beef dripping (unless for vegetarians) for greasing tins

deep bun tray

Sieve the flour into a bowl, make a well in the centre of the flour and drop in the eggs. Using a small whisk or wooden spoon, stir continuously, gradually drawing in flour from the sides, adding the milk in a steady stream at the same time. When all the flour has been mixed in, whisk in the remainder of the milk and the cool melted butter. Allow to stand for 1 hour.

Grease hot deep bun tins with oil or pure beef dripping and fill $\frac{1}{2}$–$\frac{3}{4}$ full. Bake in a hot oven, 230°C/450°F/regulo 8, for 20 minutes approx.

^vYorkshire Pudding with Olives
Grease the tins with olive oil and drop 2 or 3 stoned olives into each one.

^vMustard and Thyme Yorkshire Pudding
Alternatively add some thyme leaves to the mixture and English or French mustard to each bun tray.

Steak with Irish Whiskey and Tarragon

Serves 4

This is a quick and easy sauce for steak. Most people usually have a drop of the 'hard stuff' hidden in the cupboard, so use a little drop for this!

> **4 well-hung sirloin *or* fillet steaks**
> **1 clove of garlic**
> **lots of freshly ground pepper**
> **olive oil**
> **salt**
> **2–4 tablesp. (2$\frac{1}{2}$–5 American tablesp.) Irish whiskey**
> **4 fl ozs (100 ml/$\frac{1}{2}$ cup) homemade beef stock**
> **4 fl ozs (100 ml/$\frac{1}{2}$ cup) cream**
> **1 tablesp. (1 American tablesp. + 1 teasp.) freshly chopped**
>   **tarragon**

Cut the clove of garlic in half and rub the cut side over the steaks. Crush the garlic and reserve for the sauce. Season the steaks with freshly ground pepper and drizzle over a little olive oil.

Just before serving, heat a heavy pan. Season the steaks with salt and cook to your taste. Remove to a plate. Deglaze the pan with whiskey and allow to flame; as the flames die away, add the crushed garlic, stock, cream and tarragon. Bring to the boil and simmer for a few minutes until the sauce tastes really good and lightly coats the back of a spoon.[*]

Put the steaks on to 4 warm plates. Pour any escaped juices into the sauce, taste, correct the seasoning, spoon over the steaks and serve immediately.

*Variation

4 ozs (110 g) sautéed mushrooms may be added to the sauce at the end.

*Scalloped Potato with Steak and Kidney

Serves 4–6

This is a very economical and enormously comforting dish. We used to ask my mother to make it when we came home from college on winter weekends. You can do lots of variations on the theme; streaky bacon is particularly good and shoulder of lamb would also be delicious.

1 lb (450 g) well-hung stewing beef (I use round, flank *or* even lean shin)
1 beef kidney
salt and freshly ground pepper
$2\frac{1}{2}$–3 lbs (1.1–1.35 kg) 'old' potatoes — Golden Wonders *or* Kerr's Pinks
$\frac{3}{4}$ lb (340 g/$2\frac{1}{2}$ cups) onions, chopped
2–$2\frac{1}{2}$ ozs (55–70 g/$\frac{1}{2}$–$\frac{5}{8}$ stick) butter
water *or* homemade stock

Garnish
freshly chopped parsley

I use a large, oval Le Creuset casserole, 4 pint–2.3 L/10 cup–capacity.

Remove the skin and white core from the kidney and discard; cut the flesh into $\frac{1}{2}$ inch (1 cm) cubes, put them into a bowl, cover with cold water and sprinkle with a good pinch of salt. Cut the beef into $\frac{1}{2}$ inch (1 cm) cubes also. Peel the potatoes and cut them into $\frac{1}{4}$ inch (5 mm) thick slices. Put a layer of potato slices on the base of the casserole. Drain the kidney and mix with the beef, then scatter some of the meat and chopped onion over the layer of potato. Season well with salt and freshly ground pepper, dot with butter, add another layer of potato, more meat, onions and seasoning and continue right up to the top of the casserole. Finish with an overlapping layer of potato. Pour in the stock, 13 fl ozs (375 ml) approx. Bring to the boil, cover and cook in a preheated slow oven, 150°C/300°F/regulo 2, for 2–$2\frac{1}{2}$ hours or until the meat and potatoes are cooked. Sprinkle with chopped parsley and serve from the casserole.

We eat this in deep plates with lots and lots of butter.

You can remove the lid of the saucepan near the end of the cooking time to brown the top slightly for a more appetising appearance.

Stir-fried Beef with Oyster Sauce

Serves 6–8

Deh-ta-Hsiung came to teach a Chinese cooking course at Ballymaloe Cookery School several times, and this was one of his favourite beef recipes which we have been making ever since. A stir-fry is terrific to make a little beef go a long way.

> 12–14 ozs (350–400 g) beef steak, e.g. rump
> 1 teasp. sugar
> 1 tablesp. (1 American tablesp. + 1 teasp.) light soy sauce
> 2 tablesp. (2 American tablesp. + 2 teasp.) rice wine *or* dry sherry
> 2 teasp. cornflour, slaked with 1 tablesp. (1 American tablesp.
>   + 1 teasp.) water
> 4 ozs (110 g) bamboo shoots, sliced
> 4 ozs (110 g/scant 1 cup) carrots, sliced
> 4 ozs (110 g) baby corn cobs (optional)
> 4 ozs (110 g) broccoli *or* courgettes *or* mangetout peas *or* a mixture
> 4–5 tablesp. (5–7 American tablesp.) sunflower *or* peanut oil
> 1–2 spring onions, cut into short lengths
> 1 slice peeled ginger root
> 1 scant teasp. salt
> 1 teasp. sugar
> stock *or* water
> 2–3 tablesp. (2½–4 American tablesp.) oyster sauce

Cut the beef into thin slices about the size of a large postage stamp. Marinate with the sugar, soy sauce, wine and cornflour for 25–30 minutes. Prepare the vegetables, i.e. cut the bamboo shoots and carrots into roughly the same size as the beef; slice the broccoli or courgettes and corn cobs if using or top and tail the mangetout peas. Heat the oil in a preheated wok, stir-fry the beef for about 30–40 seconds or until the colour changes and then quickly remove with a slotted spoon. In the same oil, add the spring onion, ginger and the vegetables; stir-fry for about 2–3 minutes, then add the salt, sugar and a little stock or water if necessary; now add the beef and oyster sauce and blend well. Stir for 1 more minute and serve hot.

*Basic Hamburgers

Serves 4–6

Hamburgers are the universal fast food — eaten by rich and poor alike, a trendy snack or a cheap and hopefully nourishing staple, widely available and enormously variable! I worry greatly about the content of many of the commercially made burgers and marvel at how they can be held up and swung around without disintegrating. My homemade ones would be spattered all around the kitchen if I tried that!

I feel that many people must be unaware how easy it is to make homemade hamburgers. When buying mince for hamburgers it is not necessary to have an expensive cut of beef: chump, round or lean shin are perfect and a very little bit of fat makes it deliciously juicy. But the most important thing is to make sure that the meat is used on the day it was minced, otherwise it will go sour because the meat will have been bruised in the process of mincing. Hamburgers can be served in myriad different ways; everyone has a favourite. Here are three of ours.

> 1 lb (450 g) freshly minced beef — flank, chump *or* shin would be
>   perfect
> $\frac{1}{2}$ oz (15 g/$\frac{1}{8}$ stick) butter
> 3 ozs (85 g/$\frac{3}{4}$ cup) onions, chopped
> $\frac{1}{2}$ teasp. fresh thyme leaves
> $\frac{1}{2}$ teasp. finely chopped fresh parsley
> 1 egg, preferably free-range, beaten
> salt and freshly ground pepper
> pork caul fat* (optional)
> oil *or* dripping

Melt the butter in a saucepan and toss in the chopped onions, sweat until soft but not coloured, then allow to get cold. Meanwhile mix the mince with the herbs and beaten egg, season with salt and freshly ground pepper, add the onions and mix well. Fry off a tiny bit on the pan to check the seasoning and correct if necessary. Then shape into hamburgers, 4–6 depending on the size you require. Wrap each one in caul fat if using. Cook to your taste on a medium-hot pan in a little oil or dripping, turning once.

* Pork caul fat is available from Sean Loughnane, 56 Dominick Street, Galway, tel. (091) 64437, and other butchers around the country by request.

15

*Hamburgers with Mushroom à la Crème and Crispy Bacon

Serves 6

> 6 homemade hamburgers (see p. 15)
> 1 x recipe for Mushroom à la Crème (see below)
> 6 streaky rashers
> freshly chopped parsley
>
> sizzling chips (optional — see p. 64)
> green salad and cherry tomatoes (optional)

Cook the hamburgers to your taste. Meanwhile fry or grill the rashers until crisp and golden, then cut each one in half. Heat the Mushroom à la Crème.

Put a hamburger on each plate, spoon 1–2 tablespoons ($1\frac{1}{2}$–$2\frac{1}{2}$ American tablespoons) of Mushroom à la Crème over each. Top each hamburger with 2 pieces of crispy bacon and a sprinkling of freshly chopped parsley.

Serve with some sizzling chips and a green salad and perhaps a few cherry tomatoes.

ᵛMushroom à la Crème

Serves 4

> $\frac{1}{2}$–1 oz (15–30 g/$\frac{1}{8}$–$\frac{1}{4}$ stick) butter
> 3 ozs (85 g/$\frac{3}{4}$ cup) onions, finely chopped
> $\frac{1}{2}$ lb (225 g/$2\frac{1}{4}$ cups) mushrooms, sliced
> 1 clove of garlic (optional)
> 4 fl ozs (100 ml/$\frac{1}{2}$ cup) cream
> freshly chopped parsley
> $\frac{1}{2}$ tablesp. freshly chopped chives (optional)
> squeeze of lemon juice
> Salt and freshly ground pepper

Melt the butter in a heavy saucepan until it foams. Add the chopped onions, cover and sweat on a gentle heat for 5–10 minutes or until quite soft but not coloured; remove the onions to a bowl. Increase the heat and cook the sliced mushrooms, in batches if necessary. Season each batch with salt, freshly ground pepper and a tiny squeeze of lemon juice. Add the onions to the mushrooms in the saucepan, then add the

Tomato and Basil Soup

Steak with Irish Whiskey and Tarragon

Hamburgers with Guacamole and French Fried Onions

Lamb Chops with Mint and Butter Sauce

cream and allow to bubble for a few minutes. Taste and correct the seasoning, and add parsley and chives if used.

Note: Mushroom à la Crème may be served as a vegetable, or as a filling for vol au vents, bouchées or pancakes. It may be used as an enrichment for casseroles and stews or, by adding a little more cream or stock, may be served as a sauce with beef, lamb, chicken or veal. A crushed clove of garlic may be added when the onions are sweating.

Mushroom à la Crème keeps well in the fridge for 4–5 days.

*Hamburgers with Guacamole and French Fried Onions

Serves 6

6 homemade hamburgers (see p. 15)

ᵛGuacamole
Enough to top 6 hamburgers

1 ripe avocado
**1–2 tablesp. (1½–2½ American tablesp.) freshly squeezed lime *or*
  lemon juice**
1 tablesp. (1 American tablesp. + 1 teasp.) olive oil
**1 tablesp. (1 American tablesp. + 1 teasp.) freshly chopped
  coriander *or* flat parsley**
sea salt and freshly ground pepper

Garnish
sprig of flat parsley *or* watercress

To serve
french fried onions (see below)
sizzling chips (see p. 64)
green salad (see p. 69)

First make the Guacamole. Scoop out the flesh from the avocado. Mash with a fork, add lime juice, olive oil, chopped coriander, salt and freshly ground pepper to taste.

Fry the hamburgers on a hot pan with a very little olive oil or dripping. Lower the heat after cooking a few minutes on each side and continue until the hamburgers are to your taste. Meanwhile cook the chips and French Fried Onions.

17

To serve: Put a hamburger on to a warm plate with a portion of sizzling chips beside it. A generous tablespoonful of Guacamole goes on top and finish this off with 5 or 6 crispy French Fried Onion rings.

Quickly toss some green salad in a little French dressing and put some on to the side of the plate with 2 or 3 cherry tomatoes. Garnish with a sprig of flat parsley or watercress and serve immediately.

Note: If you would prefer to eat the Guacamole burger in a bun, split a crusty homemade burger bun in half, toast the inside, then fill with the burger, Guacamole, French Fried Onions and green salad. Open your mouth very wide and enjoy!

ᵛFrench Fried Onions

Serves 6

> **1 large onion**
> **milk**
> **seasoned white flour, preferably unbleached**
> **good quality oil** *or* **beef dripping for deep-frying**

Slice the onion into $\frac{1}{4}$ inch (5 mm) rings around the middle. Separate the rings and cover with milk until needed. Just before serving, heat the oil to 180°C/350°F. Toss the rings in seasoned flour, a few at a time. Deep-fry until golden in the hot oil.

Drain on kitchen paper and serve hot with steaks, hamburgers etc.

*Hamburgers with Blue Cheese, Sweet Cucumber Salad and Tomato Relish

Serves 4–6

> **Basic Hamburger recipe (see p. 15)**
> **little Irish Blue cheese — Cashel Blue** *or* **Chetwynd**

ᵛ ᵛᵛ Sweet Cucumber Salad

> **4 ozs (110 g) approx. cucumber, thinly sliced**
> **1 dessertsp. sugar**
> **$1\frac{1}{4}$ fl ozs (31.5 ml/generous $\frac{1}{8}$ cup) white wine vinegar**
> **good pinch of salt**

To serve
Ballymaloe Country Relish or **a good homemade tomato chutney**
green salad (see p. 70)
marigold petals (*Calendula officinalis*** — optional)**
freshly cooked chips (optional — see p. 64)

First make the cucumber salad. Put the sliced cucumber into a bowl; add the sugar, salt and wine vinegar and mix well. Place in a tightly covered container in the fridge and leave for at least half an hour.

Meanwhile make the hamburger mixture. When shaping the hamburgers put a blob of Blue cheese into the centre of each one and seal well. Cook the burgers to your taste.

To serve: Put a freshly cooked Blue cheese burger on a warm plate, arrange some cucumber salad on top, and put a spoonful of Ballymaloe Country Relish on the side. Some sizzling chips and a little tossed green salad would also be delicious. If you happen to have a few common marigold petals, sprinkle them over the top of the salad for extra posh!

* Ballymaloe Country Relish is available in shops countrywide; if it is unavailable in your area contact Yasmin Hyde, Glanmire, Co. Cork, tel. (021) 353358.

Roast Loin of Lamb with Duxelle Stuffing and Mint Sauce

Serves 10–12

Irish lamb is still remarkably sweet and for the most part naturally reared. No lamb I've tasted from any starred restaurant menus on the continent could equal the flavour of the lamb I buy from my local butcher, Michael Cuddigan, who rears his animals on rich old pastures full of wild flowers and herbs. There are still many conscientious butchers like Michael around the country, so search them out and support them.

1 whole loin of lamb (6$\frac{1}{2}$ lbs/2.9 kg approx. — allow 6–8 ozs /170–225 g
    of boned loin per person)
salt and freshly ground pepper

Duxelle Stuffing
16 ozs (450 g) mushrooms, chopped
16 ozs (450 g) ham or **bacon (cooked)**
4 ozs (110 g/1 stick) butter

19

8 ozs (225 g/1½ cups) onions, chopped
2 tablesp. (2 American tablesp. + 2 teasp.) mixed freshly chopped
    parsley, chives and fresh thyme leaves
salt and freshly ground pepper

Gravy
1 pint (600 ml/2½ cups) homemade lamb *or* chicken stock (see p. 5)
roux
1 tablesp. (1 American tablesp. + 1 teasp.) freshly chopped parsley,
    chives and thyme (optional)

First make the stuffing. Melt the butter in a saucepan and add the chopped onions. Sweat on a gentle heat until soft. Increase the heat, add the chopped mushrooms, season with salt and pepper and cook for 2–3 minutes. Add the chopped ham and herbs, taste and check the seasoning. Allow the mixture to cool before stuffing the loin of lamb.

Bone the loin of lamb. Put the bones into a saucepan with a few aromatic vegetables and a bouquet garni, bring to the boil and simmer for a few hours to make a little stock for the gravy. Lightly score the fat side, turn over and trim off the excess flap. Keep it to make Epigrams (see opposite). Sprinkle the joint with salt and freshly ground pepper. Spread the stuffing on the boned side, roll it up like a swiss roll and tie with cotton string.

Roast in a moderate oven, 180°C/350°F/regulo 4, for 1½ hours approx. When the loin is cooked, remove from the roasting pan, place on a serving dish and keep warm.

To make the gravy: Degrease the roasting tin and deglaze with the stock. Allow the stock to boil for a few minutes. Whisk in a little roux if a slightly thick gravy is preferred. Season with salt and freshly ground pepper and if you have them add perhaps a sprinkling of freshly chopped herbs.

Serve with Mint Sauce or Apple and Mint Jelly (see p. 107).

ᵛ ᵛᵛ *Mint Sauce*

1 heaped tablesp. finely chopped fresh mint
2 teasp. (10 g/2 American teasp.) sugar
2½ fl ozs (63 ml/¼ cup) boiling water
1 tablesp. (1 American tablesp. + 1 teasp.) white wine vinegar
    or lemon juice

Put the sugar and freshly chopped mint into a sauce boat. Add the boiling water and vinegar or lemon juice. Allow to infuse for 5–10 minutes before serving.

Lamb Chops Duxelle

Even a few simple lamb chops can be made into a feast with the Duxelle Stuffing.

Cut a pocket in the eye of the chops, fill with a generous teaspoonful of Duxelle Stuffing (see opposite). Dip the chops first in seasoned flour, then in beaten egg and then in breadcrumbs. Bake on an oiled baking sheet in a preheated oven, 200°C/400°F/regulo 6, for 25–30 minutes.

Epigrams

Cheap and absolutely delicious.

Remove the streaky part of the loin of lamb in one piece. Score the fat side and cut into strips about 3 inches (7.5 cm) wide. Dip into flour, then beaten egg and then crumbs. Bake in a hot oven for 40–45 minutes.

Lamb Chops with Mint and Butter Sauce

Serves 4

Simple and delicious!

> 4–8 centre *or* side loin lamb chops
> 1 tablesp. (1 American tablesp. + 1 teasp.) shallot *or* spring
>   onion, finely chopped
> 4 tablesp. (5 American tablesp.) dry white wine
> 10 fl ozs (285 ml/1¼ cups) homemade lamb *or* chicken stock (see p. 5)
> 1 tablesp. (1 American tablesp. + 1 teasp.) freshly chopped mint
> 1–2 ozs (30–55 g/¼–½ stick) butter
> salt and freshly ground pepper

> *Garnish*
> sprig of mint

Season the lamb chops with salt and freshly ground pepper. Fry until golden and cooked to your taste; keep them warm.

Pour the excess fat off the pan, add in the finely chopped shallot or spring onion and cook for 1–2 minutes, adding a tiny knob of butter if necessary; then add dry white wine and stock. Bring to the boil and scrape the bottom of the pan to dissolve the caramelised juices. Reduce to about half of the original volume, then add the freshly chopped mint. Arrange one or two lamb chops on each hot plate. Swirl the remaining butter into the sauce, taste and correct the seasoning, divide the sauce between the four plates, garnish with a sprig of mint and serve immediately.

Lamb Stew with Bacon, Onions and Garden Herbs

Serves 4–6

The word stew is often associated in these islands with not very exciting mid-week dinners. People tend to say almost apologetically, oh it's only stew, no matter how delicious it is. Well, let me tell you they smack their lips in France at the mere mention of a great big bubbling stew and now these gutsy, comforting pots are appearing on many of the smartest restaurant menus.

> **4 lbs (1.8 kg) shoulder of lamb** *or* **thick rack chops**
> **12 ozs (340 g) green streaky bacon (blanch if salty)**
> **seasoned white flour, preferably unbleached**
> **a little butter** *or* **oil for sautéeing**
> **1 lb (450 g) onions (baby ones are nicest)**
> **12 ozs (340 g) carrots, peeled and thickly sliced**
> **1¼ pints (750 ml/3 cups) approx. lamb** *or* **chicken stock (see p. 5)**
> **8–12 'old' potatoes (optional)**
> **sprig of thyme**
> **roux (optional — see p. 34)**
> **Mushroom à la Crème (optional — see p. 16)**
>
> *Garnish*
> **1 dessertsp. (2 American teasp.) freshly chopped parsley**

Cut the rind off the bacon and cut into approx. ½ inch (1 cm) cubes. Blanch if salty and dry on kitchen paper. Divide the lamb into 8 pieces and roll in seasoned flour. Heat a little oil in a frying pan and sauté the bacon until crisp, remove and put in a casserole. Add the lamb to the pan and sauté until golden, then add to the bacon in the casserole. Heat control is crucial here: the pan mustn't burn yet it must be hot enough to sauté the lamb. If it is too cool the lamb will stew rather than sauté and as a result the meat may be tough. Then quickly sauté the onions and carrots, adding a little butter if necessary, and put them into the casserole. Degrease the sauté pan and deglaze with the stock, bring to the boil and pour over the lamb.

Cover the top of the stew with peeled potatoes (if using) and season well. Add a sprig of thyme and bring to simmering point on top of the stove, then put into the oven for 45–60 minutes, 180°C/350°F/regulo 4. Cooking time depends on how long the lamb was sautéed for.

When the casserole is just cooked, strain off the cooking liquid, degrease and return degreased liquid to the casserole and bring to the boil. Thicken with a little roux if necessary. Add back in the meat, carrots and onions and potatoes if using, bring back to the boil.

The casserole is very good served at this point, but it's even more delicious if some Mushroom à la Crème is stirred in as an enrichment. Serve bubbling hot and sprinkled with chopped parsley.

Variations
1 Add $\frac{1}{2}$ lb (225 g) of precooked haricot beans to the stew about two-thirds of the way through cooking, and omit the potatoes.

2 Substitute half the Tomato Fondue recipe (see p. 68) for the Mushroom à la Crème recipe (see p. 16) and you will have a quite different but equally delicious stew.

Mild Madras Curry with Fresh Spices, with Cucumber and Yoghurt Raita and Hot Chilli Sauce

Serves 8

The word curry conjures up images of steam coming out the ears! But curries needn't necessarily be hot; this one is mildly spiced and includes no chilli. Quorma curries often include cream which comes as a surprise to many people. This particularly delicious recipe can be reheated and even freezes very well. If you enjoy a hot curry, serve the hot chilli sauce as an accompaniment.

Don't be put off by the fact that I use fresh spices here. In India people wouldn't dream of using curry powder; they would grind and blend their own spices. If fresh spices are new to you, don't worry, you'll soon become familiar with their flavours. They are no more difficult to use than fresh herbs and they will add an exotic touch to your food.

2 lbs (900 g) lean boneless lamb *or* mutton (leg *or* shoulder is perfect)

4 ozs (110 g) almonds $\bigg\}$ nut milk
½ pint (300 ml/1¼ cups) light cream
1 tablesp. (1 American tablesp. + 1 teasp.) pounded fresh green
  ginger
salt
1½ ozs (45 g) ghee *or* clarified butter (see below)
4 onions, sliced in rings
4 cloves of garlic
1 teasp. green cardamom seeds, preferably extracted from whole
  pods
2 teasp. coriander seed
2 teasp. black peppercorns
½ teasp. cloves *or* 8 whole cloves
2 dessertsp. (1 American tablesp.) turmeric powder
2 teasp. sugar
freshly squeezed lime *or* lemon juice

Blanch, peel and roughly chop the almonds (they should be the texture of nibbed almonds). Put them into a saucepan with the cream and simmer for 5 minutes. Turn off the heat and leave this nut milk to infuse for 15 minutes.

Peel the ginger thinly with a vegetable peeler, then pound it into a paste in a pestle and mortar or chop finely with a knife. Cut the meat into 1½ inch (4 cm) cubes and mix it with the ginger and a sprinkling of salt. Melt the butter in a casserole on a gentle heat, then sweat the onion rings and crushed garlic in it for 5 minutes.

Remove the seeds from the cardamom pods and measure 1 teaspoon. Discard the pods. Grind the fresh spices (coriander, pepper, cardamom and cloves) in a clean spice or coffee grinder. Add the spices to the onions and cook over a medium heat for 5 minutes.

Remove the onions and then add the meat to the saucepan. Stir over a high heat until the meat changes colour, then return the onion and spices to the pot. Add in nut milk, turmeric and sugar. Stir well. Cover and simmer gently on top of the stove or in a low oven, 160°C/325°F/regulo 3, until the meat is cooked (1 hour approx.) Finish by adding lime or lemon juice to taste.

Serve with boiled rice and other curry accompaniments which might include bowls of Ballymaloe Country Relish or mango chutney, Cucumber and Yoghurt Raita, Hot Chilli Sauce, some Indian breads, poppadums (cooked according to instructions on packet), sliced bananas, chopped apples etc.

Note: One biggish leg of lamb or mutton will yield approx. 3–4 lbs (1.35–1.8 kg) of meat. You may as well make twice the recipe, as curry keeps well and also freezes perfectly.

Clarified Butter
Melt 8 ozs (225 g/2 sticks) butter gently in a saucepan or in the oven. Allow it to stand for a few minutes, then spoon the crusty white layer of salt particles off the top of the melted butter. Underneath this crust there is clear liquid butter which is called clarified butter. The milky liquid underneath the clarified butter can be discarded or used in a white sauce.

Clarified butter is excellent for cooking because it can withstand a higher temperature when the salt and milk particles are removed. It will keep covered in a fridge for several weeks.

^v*Cucumber and Yoghurt Raita*

This cooling relish is good served with spicy food.

$\frac{1}{2}$ medium-sized cucumber
$\frac{1}{4}$ pint (150 ml/$\frac{3}{4}$ cup) plain yoghurt
$\frac{1}{2}$ tablesp. onion, finely chopped
$\frac{1}{2}$ rounded teasp. salt
$\frac{1}{2}$–1 ripe tomato, diced
1 tablesp. (1 American tablesp. + 1 teasp.) freshly chopped
    coriander leaves *or* $\frac{1}{2}$ tablesp. parsley and $\frac{1}{2}$ tablesp. mint
$\frac{1}{2}$ teasp. ground cumin seed

Peel the cucumber if you prefer, cut in half and remove the seeds, then cut into $\frac{1}{4}$ inch (5 mm) dice. Put this into a bowl with the onion, sprinkle with salt and allow to degorge for 5–10 minutes. Drain, add the diced tomato and the chopped coriander, or parsley and mint, to the yoghurt. Heat the cumin seeds, crush lightly and add to the Raita. Taste and correct the seasoning. Chill before serving.

^{v vv}*Hot Chilli Sauce*

If you want some real excitement in your life, eat large spoonfuls of this with your curry! We use it as a basis for Chilli con Carne as well.

4–5 fresh chillies *or* 6–7 small dried chillies
1 large onion
1 large red pepper

2 cloves of garlic
salt

Cut the chillies and pepper in half and wash out the seeds. If the chillies are dried, soak them for about an hour, then split them in half and wash out the seeds.

Purée with the other ingredients in a food processor. You may need 1 or 2 tablespoons of cold water if the mixture is too dry. Season to taste with salt. This sauce can be stored in a covered container for a few days, or it can be frozen for much longer.

Note: Salt brings up the flavour of chillies so don't forget to put it in.

*Roast Stuffed Fillet of Pork with Apple Sauce

Serves 6–8

It seems to me that the flavour of pork has suffered from mass production possibly even more than any other meat. It becomes increasingly difficult to find pork that is sweet and juicy as one remembers it as a child, and the problem is compounded by the mania for lean meat. I would encourage more pig farmers to abandon the almost impossible task of producing pork economically under the present system and to revert to rearing pigs more naturally. Those who have done so have discovered that they can provide excellent pork quite economically; because their animals are so healthy they need virtually no antibiotics or other medicines.

2 pork fillets, naturally produced if available
salt and freshly ground pepper
$\frac{1}{2}$–1 oz (15–30 g/$\frac{1}{8}$ – $\frac{1}{4}$ stick) butter

Stuffing
6 ozs (170 g/1$\frac{1}{2}$ cups) onions, chopped
3 ozs (85 g/$\frac{3}{4}$ stick) butter
6 ozs (170 g/3 cups approx.) soft white breadcrumbs (see below)
4 tablesp. (5 American tablesp.) freshly chopped herbs — parsley, thyme, chives, marjoram and perhaps a very little sage *or* rosemary
salt and freshly ground pepper

or **Potato and Apple Stuffing (use half the recipe below)**
large needle and cotton thread

Gravy
$\frac{3}{4}$ pint (450 ml/generous 1$\frac{1}{2}$ cups) chicken stock (see p. 5)

26

First make the stuffing. Sweat the onions gently in butter for 5–6 minutes. When they are soft, stir in the breadcrumbs (see method for making them below), the herbs and a little salt and freshly ground pepper to taste. Allow to get quite cold.

Preheat the oven to 220°C/425°F/regulo 7. Trim the pork fillets of fat and gristle. Slit each one down one side and open out; flatten slightly with a mallet or rolling pin. Season with salt and freshly ground pepper.

Cover one fillet with stuffing and top with the other fillet. Sew the edges with cotton thread.

Smear the top with soft butter and roast in the preheated oven for 30 minutes approx., depending on the size of the fillets. After 20 minutes turn the pork over and baste so that the base browns also. When cooked, transfer to a carving plate and allow to rest while you make the gravy.

Degrease the pan juices if necessary, add $\frac{3}{4}$ pint (450 ml) chicken stock to the roasting pan and bring to the boil, using a whisk to dislodge the caramelised juices from the pan. Continue to simmer for a few minutes, taste and add seasoning if necessary. Pour into a hot sauce boat. Slice the pork into thick slices, $\frac{1}{2}$ inch (1 cm) approx. Serve with Apple Sauce (see below), gravy and lots of crusty roast potatoes.

For details of Olivia Goodwillie's pork circle, supplied from Lavistown, Co. Kilkenny, tel. (056) 65145.

Breadcrumbs
Cut the crusts off good quality stale white bread and whizz the soft part of the bread in the liquidiser or food processor for a few seconds. Breadcrumbs can be frozen and used directly from the freezer — an essential standby in my opinion. Crusts may be left on if you don't mind slightly brown crumbs, or they may be dried out and then ground up and sieved for dry breadcrumbs. Use for Cheddar Cheese Croquettes (see p. 44). Dried breadcrumbs will keep for weeks in a screw-top jar.

Suggested alternative stuffings: Potato and Apple Stuffing or Duxelle Stuffing (see p. 19).

^v*Potato and Apple Stuffing*

    1 lb (450 g) potatoes
    1 oz (30 g/$\frac{1}{4}$ stick) butter
    $\frac{1}{2}$ lb (225 g/1$\frac{1}{2}$ cups) onions, chopped

$\frac{1}{2}$ lb (225 g) Bramley Seedling cooking apples, peeled and chopped
$\frac{1}{2}$ tablesp. freshly chopped parsley
$\frac{1}{2}$ tablesp. freshly chopped lemon balm
salt and freshly ground pepper

Boil the unpeeled potatoes in salted water until cooked, peel and mash. Melt the butter and sweat the onions in a covered saucepan on a gentle heat for about 5 minutes. Add the apples and cook until they break down into a fluff, then stir in the mashed potatoes and herbs. Season with salt and freshly ground pepper. Allow to get quite cold before stuffing the pork.

ᵛApple sauce

Serves 8

> 1 lb (450 g) cooking apples, Bramley Seedling *or* Grenadier
> 2 ozs (55 g/$\frac{1}{4}$ cup approx.) sugar (depending on how tart the apples are)
> 1–2 dessertsp. (2–4 American teasp.) water

Peel, quarter and core the apples; cut the pieces in two and put them in a stainless steel or cast-iron saucepan, with the sugar and water. Cover and cook on a very low heat until the apples break down into a fluff. Stir and taste for sweetness.

Serve warm or cold.

Carbonnade of Pork

Serves 6–8

A quick and delicious recipe, whose formula can be used for fillet steak or chicken breast but be careful not to overcook the meat. If you haven't got any wine to hand just add a little more stock.

> 2 lbs (900 g) pork fillet, naturally reared if available
> 1–2 tablesp. (1$\frac{1}{2}$–2$\frac{1}{2}$ American tablesp.) olive *or* sunflower oil
>   *or* a little butter
> 4 ozs (110 g/scant 1 cup) onions, finely chopped
> 2$\frac{1}{2}$ fl ozs (63 ml/generous $\frac{1}{4}$ cup) dry white wine
> $\frac{1}{4}$ pint (150 ml/generous $\frac{1}{2}$ cup) homemade chicken stock (see p. 5)
> 8 ozs (225 g/4 cups) mushrooms, sliced
> $\frac{1}{2}$ pint (300 ml/1$\frac{1}{4}$ cups) sour cream *or* light cream

a little roux
fresh lemon juice
salt and freshly ground pepper
2 tablesp. (2 American tablesp. + 2 teasp.) freshly chopped parsley

Garnish
6–8 heart-shaped croûtons of white bread fried in clarified butter
    or **olive oil**

Cut the pork into slices about $\frac{1}{3}$ inch (8 mm) thick. Pour a little oil into a very hot frying pan, sauté the pieces of pork a few at a time until brown on both sides. Remove to a plate and keep warm. Add a little more oil or butter and cook the onions gently until soft and golden. Deglaze the pan with wine and bring to the boil, add the stock and boil again to reduce by one-quarter. Meanwhile sauté the sliced mushrooms a few at a time in a little butter and oil in a very hot frying pan; add to the pork. Add the cream to the onions and stock, bring back to the boil, thicken slightly with a little roux then add the cooked pork and mushrooms to the sauce with all the juices. Taste, add a little freshly squeezed lemon juice and simmer gently for a couple of minutes.*

For extra posh, dip the tip of each heart-shaped croûton into the sauce and then into the chopped parsley, add the remainder of the parsley to the sauce, taste again and correct seasoning if necessary. Pour into a hot serving dish, garnish with crisp croûtons and serve immediately.

* Can be prepared ahead to this point.

Homemade Sausages with Apple Sauce

Makes 16 approx.

Homemade sausages are just as easy to make as hamburgers and make a cheap and comforting meal.

1 lb (450 g) streaky pork
1–2 teasp. freshly chopped mixed herbs — parsley, thyme, chives,
    marjoram and rosemary *or* **sage**
$2\frac{1}{2}$ ozs (70 g/generous 1 cup) soft white breadcrumbs
1 clove of garlic
1 egg, preferably free-range
salt and freshly ground pepper
a little oil

Apple Sauce (see opposite)

29

Mince the pork. Chop the herbs finely and mix through the crumbs. Crush the garlic to a paste with a little salt. Whisk the egg, then mix all the ingredients together thoroughly. Season with salt and freshly ground pepper. Fry off a little knob of the mixture to check the seasoning, correct if necessary. Divide into 16 pieces and roll into lengths. Fry gently on a barely oiled pan until golden on all sides. They are particularly delicious served with red cabbage and Apple Sauce and perhaps a big bowl of buttery champ or colcannon.

Traditional Roast Stuffed Chicken with Parsley Sauce

Serves 4–6

A crispy roast free-range chicken with lots of gravy and a good stuffing is everyone's idea of a real feast. Many of us have forgotten how easy it is to make stuffing, it only takes a few minutes, particularly if you keep some breadcrumbs in the freezer (see p. 27).

1 free-range chicken, $3\frac{1}{2}$ – 5 lbs (1.5–2.3 kg)

Stock
giblets, wing tips and wish bone (keep the liver for a chicken liver pâté)
1 sliced carrot
1 sliced onion
1 stick celery
few parsley stalks and a sprig of thyme

Stuffing
$1\frac{1}{2}$ ozs (45 g/3 tablesp.) butter
3 ozs (85 g/$\frac{3}{4}$ cup) chopped onion
3–$3\frac{1}{2}$ ozs (85–100 g/$1\frac{1}{2}$–$1\frac{3}{4}$ cups) soft white breadcrumbs
2 tablesp. (2 American tablesp. + 2 teasp.) finely chopped fresh herbs — parsley, lemon thyme, chives and annual marjoram
salt and freshly ground pepper
a little soft butter

Garnish
sprigs of flat parsley

First remove the wishbone from the neck end of the chicken; this isn't at all essential but it does make carving much easier later on. Tuck the wing tips underneath the chicken to make a neat shape.

To make the stock, put the wish bone, giblets, carrot, onions, celery and herbs into a saucepan. Cover with cold water, bring to the boil, skim and simmer gently while the chicken is roasting.

Next make the stuffing. Sweat the onions gently in the butter until soft (10 minutes approx.), then stir in the crumbs, freshly chopped herbs, a little salt and pepper to taste. Allow it to get quite cold.

If necessary wash and dry the cavity of the bird, then season and half fill with cold stuffing. Season the breast and legs and smear with a little soft butter. Preheat the oven to 180°C/350°F/regulo 4. Weigh the chicken and allow about 20 minutes to the pound and 20 minutes over. Half way through the cooking turn the chicken upside down to allow the juices to run into the breast. Baste a couple of times with the buttery juices.

The chicken is done when the juices are running clear. To test prick the thickest part at the base of the thigh and examine the juices: they should be clear. Remove the chicken to a carving dish, keep it warm and allow to rest while you make the gravy.

To make the gravy, spoon off the surplus fat from the roasting pan. Deglaze the pan juices with the fat-free stock from the giblets and bones (you will need $\frac{3}{4}$–1 pint depending on the size of the chicken). Using a whisk, stir and scrape well to dissolve the caramelised meat juices from the roasting pan. Boil it up well, season and thicken with a little roux if you like. Taste and correct seasoning. Serve in a hot gravy boat.

If possible serve the chicken on a nice carving dish surrounded by crispy roast potatoes and some sprigs of flat parsley, then arm yourself with a sharp knife and bring it to the table. Carve as best you can and ignore rude remarks if you are still practising, but do try to organise it so that each person gets some brown and some white meat. Serve with gravy.

We love a piece of boiled streaky bacon with roast chicken. A 3 lb (1.35 kg) piece will take 1 hour approx. to cook. Start it off in cold water and change the water several times, particularly if the bacon is salty. A skewer should go through the bacon easily when it is cooked and the skin should peel off without resistance. I then sprinkle the fat with a few toasted and sieved dry breadcrumbs (see p. 27).

ᵛ Parsley Sauce

$1\frac{1}{2}$–2 tablesp. (2–$2\frac{1}{2}$ American tablesp.) finely chopped fresh parsley
1 pint (600 ml/$2\frac{1}{2}$ cups) fresh milk
1–$1\frac{1}{2}$ ozs (30–45 g) roux (see p. 34)
salt and freshly ground pepper

Remove the stalks from the parsley, put the stalks into a saucepan with the cold milk, bring slowly to the boil, then remove the stalks. Thicken by whisking roux into the boiling milk; add the parsley. Season with salt and freshly ground pepper. Simmer for 5–10 minutes on a very low heat, taste and correct the seasoning.

Chicken Cordon Bleu

Serves 4

This classic recipe makes a very substantial main course which every-body seems to like.

> 4 chicken breasts, free-range if possible
> salt and freshly ground pepper
> French mustard
> 4 slices Irish Cheddar *or* Gruyère cheese
> 2–3 teasp. freshly chopped parsley
> 4 slices cooked ham *or* 4 cooked streaky rashers
> seasoned white flour, preferably unbleached
> beaten egg
> fine dry breadcrumbs

Detach the 'fillet' from the chicken breasts and keep aside for another recipe.

Carefully slit the chicken breast down the side and open out. Season with salt and freshly ground pepper. Smear with a little French mustard, put a thin slice of Irish Cheddar lengthways on one side of the chicken breast, sprinkle with a little chopped parsley, and top with a slice of cooked ham or cooked streaky rasher. Fold over the other side of each chicken breast, and press well to seal.

Dip each one first in seasoned flour, then into beaten egg and then fine dry breadcrumbs. Press well again.

Fry until golden and cooked all the way through in some clarified butter in a shallow pan, or deep fry in good quality oil at 160°C/325°F for 10–15 minutes depending on the size of the chicken breasts.

Serve immediately.

Gratin Dauphinois (see p. 61) and Piperonata (see p. 69) or Tomato Fondue (see p. 68) are particularly delicious accompaniments.

Mild Madras Curry with Fresh Spices

Roast Stuffed Fillet of Pork with Apple Sauce

Irish Cheddar Cheese Croquettes

A Warm Salad of Irish Goat's Cheese with Walnut Oil Dressing

Almspurses with Tomato Sauce

*Shanagarry Chicken Casserole

Serves 4–6

Even though it may sound 'old hat', a good chicken casserole always gets a hearty welcome from my family and friends. Sometimes I make an entire meal in a pot by covering the top with whole peeled potatoes just before it goes into the oven.

1 x 3½ lb (1.57 kg) chicken, preferably free-range
12 ozs (340 g) green streaky bacon (blanch if salty)
seasoned flour
a little butter *or* oil for sautéeing
1 lb (450 g) onions (baby onions are nicest)
12 ozs (340 g) carrots, peeled and thickly sliced
sprig of thyme
1¼ pints (750 ml) approx. homemade chicken stock (see p. 5)
roux (optional — see below)
Mushroom à la Crème (optional — see p. 16)

Garnish
1 dessertsp. (2 American teasp.) freshly chopped parsley

Cut the rind off the bacon and cut into approx. ½ inch (1 cm) cubes, (blanch if salty). Dry in kitchen paper. Joint the chicken into 8 pieces and roll in seasoned flour. Heat a little oil in a frying pan and cook the bacon until crisp, remove and transfer to the casserole.

Add chicken pieces a few at a time to the pan and sauté until golden, add to the bacon in the casserole. Heat control is crucial here: the pan mustn't burn yet it must be hot enough to sauté the chicken. If it is too cool, the chicken pieces will stew rather than sauté and as a result the meat may be tough. Then toss the onions and carrots in the pan, adding a little butter if necessary; add to the casserole.

Degrease the pan and deglaze with stock, bring to the boil and pour over the chicken. Season well, add a sprig of thyme and bring to simmering point on top of the stove, then put into the oven for 30–45 minutes, 180°C/350°F/regulo 4. Cooking time depends on how long the chicken pieces were sautéed for.

When the casserole is just cooked, strain off the cooking liquid, degrease, return the degreased liquid to the casserole and bring to the boil. Thicken with a little roux if necessary (see below). Add the meat, carrots and onions back into the casserole and bring to the boil.

The casserole is very good served at this point, but it's even more delicious if some Mushroom à la Crème (see p. 16) is stirred in as an enrichment. Serve bubbling hot, sprinkled with chopped parsley.

Roux

> **4 ozs (110 g/1 stick) butter**
> **4 ozs (110 g/scant 1 cup) white flour, preferably unbleached**

Melt the butter and cook the flour in it for 2 minutes on a low heat, stirring occasionally. Use as required. Roux can be stored in a cool place and used when needed or it can be made up on the spot if preferred. It will keep for at least a fortnight in a fridge.

Pheasant Casserole

Substitute pheasant for chicken in the recipe above.

*Shanagarry Chicken Casserole with Herb Crust

> **Shanagarry Chicken Casserole recipe as above**
>
> $\frac{1}{2}$ **Soda Bread with Herbs recipe (see p. 92)**
> **egg wash**
> **grated Cheddar cheese (optional)**

Roll out the dough into a $\frac{3}{4}$ inch (2 cm) thick round, stamp into smaller rounds with a 2 inch (5 cm) cutter. When the casserole is almost cooked remove the lid and cover the top of the stew with slightly overlapping herb scones, brush with egg wash and sprinkle with a little cheese if you wish. Increase the heat to 230°C/450°F/regulo 8 for 10 minutes, then reduce the heat to 200°C/400°F/regulo 6 for a further 20 minutes or until the crust is baked.

Spiced Chicken with Almonds

Serves 6–8

I first came across this recipe in Joyce Molyneux's *Carved Angel* cookery book; she had adapted it from a recipe in Madhur Jaffrey's *Indian Cookery* book. Joyce uses both brown and white chicken meat but it's also very good just with chicken breast.

2 lbs (900 g) boned chicken, cut into finger-sized pieces
1 tablesp. (1 American tablesp. + 1 teasp.) coriander seeds
1 tablesp. (1 American tablesp. + 1 teasp.) cumin seeds
$\frac{1}{2}$ teasp. ground turmeric
good pinch of cayenne pepper
2 teasp. salt
1 teasp. sugar
4 ozs (110 g) onions, roughly chopped
1 inch (2.5 cm) piece of fresh ginger root, sliced
3 cloves of garlic, crushed
1 oz (30 g) blanched almonds
12 ozs (340 g) red pepper, seeded and coarsely chopped
7 tablesp. (9 American tablesp.) sunflower oil
8 fl ozs (250 ml/1 cup) water
2 tablesp. (2 American tablesp. + 2 teasp.) freshly squeezed lemon
   juice

First prepare the chicken. Grind the coriander and cumin in a spice grinder. Mix with turmeric, cayenne, salt, sugar, onions, ginger, garlic, almonds and peppers. Whizz in a food processor until smooth. Heat the oil in a wide sauté pan and cook the paste for about 10 minutes until reduced. Add the chicken, water and lemon juice, cover and cook gently for 15 minutes or until the chicken is tender. Serve with pilaff rice.

Note: If you would like a hotter curry, increase the amount of cayenne pepper to $\frac{1}{2}$ teaspoonful.

Fish

Everybody knows by now that I'm absolutely mad about fish! So determined am I to convert other people to scrumptious seafood that I have already devoted a whole television series and book to the subject of *Simply Delicious Fish*. The recipes I've chosen for *Simply Delicious Food for Family & Friends* are quick, easy, and guaranteed (I think!) to win over even the reluctant fish eaters that still lurk in some households.

Pangrilled Fish with Parsley Butter and Tomato Fondue

Serves 4 as main course

A piece of perfectly cooked pangrilled fish is hard to beat but it takes more care and skill than you might think to get it just right. A grill pan is a cast-iron frying pan with ridges. I pride myself in not being a gadget person but I find this piece of kitchen equipment indispensable not only for fish but also for meat, vegetables and even polenta.

> **8 fillets of very fresh fish, e.g. mackerel, grey sea mullet *or* sea bass**
> **(allow 6 ozs/170 g fish for main course, 3 ozs/85 g for a starter)**
> **seasoned white flour, preferably unbleached**
> **small knob of butter**
> $\frac{1}{2}$ **Tomato Fondue recipe (see p. 68)**
>
> *Parsley Butter*
> **2 ozs (55 g/$\frac{1}{2}$ stick) butter**
> **4 teasp. finely chopped fresh parsley**
> **a few drops of freshly squeezed lemon juice**
>
> *Garnish*
> **segments of lemon**
> **parsley**
>
> **grill pan**

First make the Parsley Butter. Cream the butter, add in the parsley and a few drops of lemon juice at a time. Roll into butter pats or form into a roll and wrap in greaseproof paper or tin foil, screwing each end so that it looks like a cracker. Refrigerate to harden.

Heat the grill pan. Dip the fish fillets in flour which has been seasoned with salt and freshly ground pepper. Shake off the excess flour and then spread a little butter with a knife on the flesh side, as though you were buttering a slice of bread rather meanly.

When the grill is quite hot but not smoking, place the fish fillets butter side down on the grill; the fish should sizzle as soon as they touch the pan. Turn down the heat slightly and let them cook for 4 or 5 minutes on that side before you turn them over. Continue to cook on the other side until crisp and golden.

Meanwhile heat the Tomato Fondue. Serve the fish on a hot plate, spoon some Tomato Fondue over each fillet, put a blob of Parsley Butter on each and serve immediately. The Parsley Butter may be served directly on the fish, or if you have a pretty shell, e.g. a gigas oyster shell, place it at the side of the plate as a container for the butter. Garnish with parsley and a segment of lemon.

Note: Fillets of any small fish are delicious pangrilled in this way. Fish under 2 lbs (900 g) such as mackerel, herring and brown trout can also be grilled whole on the pan. Fish over 2 lbs (900 g) can be filleted first and then cut across into portions. Large fish 4–6 lbs (1.8–2.7 kg) can also be grilled whole. Cook them for 10–15 minutes approx. on each side and then put in a hot oven for another 15 minutes or so to finish cooking.

Cod with Mushrooms and Buttered Crumbs

Serves 6–8 as main course

Fresh fish with a crunchy topping in a creamy sauce is always tempting. There is an added bonus with this recipe because one can do many variations, all of which are delicious.

$2\frac{1}{4}$ lbs (1.1 kg) hake, cod, ling, haddock, grey sea mullet *or* pollock
salt and freshly ground pepper
$\frac{1}{2}$ oz (15 g/$\frac{1}{8}$ stick) butter

Mornay Sauce
1 pint (600 ml/$2\frac{1}{2}$ cups) milk
few slices of carrot and onion
3 *or* 4 peppercorns
sprig of thyme and parsley
2 ozs (55 g) approx. roux (see p. 34)
5–6 ozs (140–170 g/$1\frac{1}{4}$–$1\frac{1}{2}$ cups) grated Cheddar cheese or 3 ozs
(85 g/$\frac{3}{4}$ cup) grated Parmesan cheese

$\frac{1}{4}$ teasp. mustard, preferably Dijon
salt and freshly ground pepper

Buttered Crumbs
2 ozs (55 g/$\frac{1}{2}$ stick) butter
4 ozs (110 g/2 cups) soft white breadcrumbs (see p. 27)
8 ozs (225 g) mushrooms
$\frac{1}{2}$ oz (15 g/$\frac{1}{8}$ stick) butter
1 tablesp. (1 American tablesp. + 1 teasp.) freshly chopped parsley
    (optional)
salt and freshly ground pepper

1$\frac{3}{4}$ lbs (790 g) Duchesse Potato (see *Simply Delicious 1*, p. 27)

First make the Mornay Sauce. Put the cold milk into a saucepan with a few slices of carrot and onion, 3 or 4 peppercorns and a sprig of thyme and parsley. Bring to the boil, simmer for 4–5 minutes, remove from the heat and leave to infuse for 10 minutes if you have enough time.

Strain out the vegetables, bring the milk back to the boil and thicken with roux to a light coating consistency. Add the mustard and two-thirds of the grated cheese; keep the remainder of the cheese for sprinkling over the top. Season with salt and freshly ground pepper, taste and correct the seasoning if necessary. Add the parsley if using.

Next make the buttered crumbs. Melt the butter in a pan and stir in the breadcrumbs. Remove from the heat immediately and allow to cool.

Slice the mushrooms, melt the butter and sauté them on a very hot pan, season with salt and freshly ground pepper, add the chopped parsley and keep aside.

Skin the fish and cut into portions: 6 ozs (170 g) for a main course, 3 ozs (85 g) for a starter. Season with salt and freshly ground pepper. Lay the pieces of fish in a lightly buttered ovenproof dish, sprinkle with cooked mushrooms and coat with the Mornay Sauce. Mix the remaining grated cheese with the buttered crumbs and sprinkle over the top. Pipe a ruff of fluffy Duchesse Potato around the edge if you want to have a whole meal in one dish.

Cook in a moderate oven, 180°C/350°F/regulo 4, for 25–30 minutes or until the fish is cooked through and the top is golden brown and crispy. If necessary, flash under the grill for a minute or two before you serve, to brown the edges of the potato.

Note: Cod with Mushrooms and Buttered Crumbs may be served in individual dishes. Scallop shells are very attractive, are completely ovenproof and may be used over and over again.

Variations
1   Sweat 1 lb (450 g) finely sliced leeks in 1 oz (30 g) butter in a covered casserole over a gentle heat and use instead of mushrooms.
2   Peel and sweat 1 small cucumber, cut into $\frac{1}{2}$ inch (1 cm) dice, in a little butter. Add 1–2 teaspoonsful dill or fennel. Use instead of mushrooms.
3   Put a layer of Tomato Fondue (see p. 68) under or over the fish and proceed as in the master recipe.
4   Put a layer of Pipcronata (see p. 69) under or over the fish and proceed as in the master recipe.

Scallop Shell of Seafood

Serves 8–16 (can be served as a starter or main course)

This is one of our most useful master recipes because you can make it with whatever fresh fish you can find. It will taste slightly different every time but will always be delicious.

> $2\frac{3}{4}$–3 lbs (1.2–1.3 kg) skinned fillets of fish, one type *or* a mixture —
>   cod, grey sea mullet, hake, ling, salmon, haddock *or* pollock
> 1 oz (30 g/$\frac{1}{4}$ stick) butter
> 2 tablesp. (2 American tablesp. + 2 teasp.) finely chopped shallots *or*
>   mild onions
> salt and freshly ground pepper
> fish stock *or* a mixture of dry white wine and fish stock (see *Simply*
>   *Delicious Fish*, p. 1) to cover
> creamy milk
> roux (see p. 34)
> 24–32 cooked and peeled shrimps *or* 16 cooked and peeled prawns,
>   cut in half (optional)
> 32 cooked mussels (save cooking liquid for sauce)
> 2–3 tablesp. ($2\frac{1}{2}$–4 American tablesp.) Hollandaise Sauce (optional —
>   see *Simply Delicious 1*, p. 18)
> Duchesse Potato (see *Simply Delicious 1*, p. 27)
> buttered crumbs (see p. 27) and grated cheese

Choose a wide stainless steel or cast-iron pan or saucepan, melt the butter and sweat the onions gently for a few minutes. Cut the fish into pieces 4 x 4 inches (10 x 10 cm) approx. Season with salt and freshly

39

ground pepper and arrange in a single layer on top of the shallots. Cover with fish stock and dry white wine. Cover the saucepan and simmer very gently for 4–10 minutes, depending on the thickness of the pieces of fish (be very careful not to overcook at this stage). Remove the fish carefully and divide between individual serving dishes or large scallop shells (be careful not to put too much fish into each shell or the proportion of sauce to fish will be wrong).

Bring the fish cooking liquid to the boil and reduce to about half the quantity. Add about an equal volume of creamy milk, boil again for 3–4 minutes, add the mussel cooking liquid if available, thicken to a light coating consistency with roux, take off the heat, whisk in a few spoons of Hollandaise Sauce if liked, taste and correct seasoning.

To assemble: Divide the mussels and cooked prawns or shrimps between the dishes or shells. Coat generously with the sauce, pipe a border of Duchesse Potato around each dish or shell and sprinkle the centre with a mixture of grated white Cheddar cheese and buttered crumbs.

Bake in a moderate oven for 15–30 minutes, depending on size; they should be hot and bubbly and the potato should be golden brown at the edges. Flash under a hot grill for a few seconds before serving if necessary.

Alternative way of serving: Sometimes at Ballymaloe we do not use breadcrumbs and cheese but instead when the scallop shell is hot we spoon a little Hollandaise Sauce on to the top and flash under the grill until golden.

Note: Scallop Shell of Seafood can be kept in the fridge for several days or frozen for a few weeks.

Eggs, Cheese and Pancakes

Even when the fridge and store cupboard are pretty much bare, there are usually a few eggs, some flour and butter, a drop of milk and, if you're lucky, a bit of cheese lurking in a corner. I love a challenge and I've made many delicious meals with just those ingredients and perhaps a few fresh herbs. In fact I never fail to be amazed at the marvellous repertoire of recipes that can be created, with a little imagination, out of almost nothing. Egg and cheese dishes are terrific for family cooking — fast and easy to prepare, nourishing and versatile. Many of the recipes in this section are marked with a ^V symbol to indicate that they are suitable for vegetarians (provided they are non-vegans). Vegans should search out cheese made from vegetarian rennet (see p. 88).

Free-range eggs make all the difference, of course, to the flavour of these and any other dishes requiring eggs. If I had my way everybody in Ireland would have a few hens in a corner of the garden to recycle household scraps!

^v*French Omelette

Serves 1

An omelette is the ultimate instant food but many a travesty is served in its name. The whole secret is to have the pan hot enough and to use clarified butter if at all possible (see p. 25). Ordinary butter will burn if your pan is as hot as it ought to be. The omelette should be made in half the time it takes to read this recipe. Your first may not be a joy to behold but persevere: practice makes perfect!

    2 eggs, preferably free-range
    1 dessertsp. (2 American teasp.) water *or* milk
    salt and freshly ground pepper
    1 dessertsp. (2 American teasp.) clarified butter (see p. 25) *or* olive oil

    omelette pan, preferably non-stick, 9-inch (23 cm) diameter

41

Warm a plate in the oven. Whisk the eggs with the water or milk in a bowl, using a fork or whisk, until thoroughly mixed but not too fluffy. Season with salt and freshly ground pepper. Put the warm plate beside the cooker.

Heat the omelette pan over a high heat, add the clarified butter and as soon as it sizzles, pour in the egg mixture. It will start to cook immediately, so quickly pull the edges of the omelette towards the centre with a metal spoon or spatula, tilting the pan so that the un-cooked egg runs to the sides. Continue until most of the egg is set and will not run any more, then leave the omelette to cook for a further 10 seconds to brown the bottom.

If you are using a filling, spoon the hot mixture in a line along the centre at this point.

To fold the omelette: Flip the edge just below the handle of the pan into the centre, then hold the pan almost perpendicular over the plate so that the omelette will flip over again, then half roll half slide the omelette on to the plate so that it lands folded into three. (It should not take more than 30 seconds in all to make the omelette, perhaps 45 if you are adding a filling.) Serve immediately.

Suggested Fillings
Tomato Fondue (see p. 68)
Piperonata (see p. 69)
Mushroom à la Crème (see p. 16)
Fines herbes — add 1 teasp. each of freshly chopped parsley, chives, chervil and tarragon to the eggs just before cooking.
Crispy bacon or diced cooked ham
Cheese — Cheddar, goat's, Gruyère, Parmesan or a mixture
Kidney — cook one cleaned and diced lamb kidney gently in a little butter, add 1 teaspoon of finely chopped fresh parsley; keep warm.
Smoked salmon or smoked mackerel — add about 1 oz (30 g).

^v*Macaroni Cheese*

Serves 6

Macaroni Cheese is one of my children's favourite supper dishes. We often add some cubes of cooked bacon or ham to the sauce with the cooked macaroni.

> **8 ozs (225 g/2½ cups) macaroni**
> **4 pints (2.3 L/10 cups) water**

42

1 teasp. salt
2 ozs (55 g/$\frac{1}{2}$ stick) butter
2 ozs (55 g/$\frac{1}{2}$ cup) white flour, preferably unbleached
1$\frac{1}{2}$ pints (900 ml/3$\frac{3}{4}$ cups) boiling milk
$\frac{1}{4}$ teasp. Dijon mustard
1 tablesp. (1 American tablesp. + 1 teasp.) freshly chopped parsley
(optional)
salt and freshly ground pepper
5 ozs (145 g/1$\frac{1}{2}$ cups) grated mature Cheddar cheese (I use our local
Cheddar which is made at Mitchelstown and matured at Imokilly
Creamery. Old Charleville is also excellent. See also p. 88)

pie dish, 2 pint (1.1 L)

Bring 4 pints (2.3 L/10 cups) of water to the boil with the salt. Sprinkle in the macaroni and stir to make sure it doesn't stick together. Cook until just soft, 10–15 minutes approx. Drain well.

Meanwhile melt the butter, add in the flour and cook, stirring occasionally for 1–2 minutes; remove from the heat. Whisk in the milk gradually, bring back to the boil, stirring all the time. Add the mustard, parsley if used and cheese, season with salt and freshly ground pepper to taste. Add back in the cooked macaroni, bring back to the boil and serve immediately.

Macaroni Cheese reheats very successfully provided the pasta is not overcooked in the first place. It is very good served with cold meat, particularly ham.

^v*Cheddar Cheese Soufflé with Chives*

Serves 6–8

Many people are convinced that making a soufflé is far beyond them. Not a bit of it! If you can master a white sauce, whisk egg whites stiffly into a fluffy mass and fold them gently, then you can make a soufflé that will draw gasps of admiration from your family and friends. Cheddar Cheese Soufflé does not rise to quite the heights of a Gruyère and Parmesan soufflé but it is nonetheless a very tasty supper dish or a delicious starter.

6 ozs (170 g/1$\frac{1}{2}$ cups) mature Irish Cheddar cheese, grated (see p. 88)
1 oz (30 g/$\frac{1}{4}$ stick) butter

2 tablesp. (2 American tablesp. + 2 teasp.) white flour, preferably
  unbleached
$\frac{1}{2}$ pint (300 ml/1$\frac{1}{4}$ cups) milk
3 egg yolks, preferably free-range
1 level teasp. salt
$\frac{1}{2}$ teasp. Dijon mustard
1 tablesp. (1 American tablesp. + 1 teasp.) finely chopped fresh
  chives
4 egg whites, preferably free-range

soufflé dish, 1 pint (600 ml/2$\frac{1}{2}$ cup capacity *or* 6–8 individual soufflé
  dishes

Melt the butter in a heavy saucepan; when it has stopped foaming add
the flour and stir well. Cook gently for 2 minutes. Remove the saucepan
from the heat, whisk in the milk slowly, return to the heat and cook
until the sauce boils and thickens. Remove from the heat once more and
beat in the egg yolks one by one. Then add the salt, mustard, chives and
all but 2 tablespoons of the cheese (reserved to sprinkle over the top).*

Whisk the egg whites until they reach a stiff peak. Stir about one-third
of the whites into the cheese mixture and fold in the remainder very
carefully. Put into a buttered and crumbed soufflé dish or dishes.

Sprinkle grated cheese on top and bake in a preheated oven, 200°C/
400°F/regulo 6, for 9–10 minutes for individual soufflés, or 180°C/
350°F/regulo 4 for 1 hour for a larger soufflé. They should be well risen
and golden on top yet slightly soft in the centre.

Serve immediately on hot plates.

* Can be prepared ahead to this stage but the base mixture must be
warmed gently before egg whites are folded in.

Note: Egg whites must not be whisked until you are about to cook the
soufflé, otherwise they will lose volume.

ᵛ*Irish Cheddar Cheese Croquettes

Makes 50–60, depending on size

We get into big trouble if these crispy cheese croquettes are not on the
Ballymaloe lunch buffet every Sunday. They are loved by children and
grown-ups, and are a particular favourite with vegetarians. They are
not suitable for vegans.

8 ozs (225 g/2$\frac{1}{2}$ cups) grated mature Cheddar cheese (I use
   Mitchelstown; see also p. 88)
15 fl ozs (450 ml/scant 2 cups) milk
few slices of carrot and onion
1 small bay leaf
sprig of thyme
4 parsley stalks
8 ozs (225 g/1 cup) roux (see p. 34)
2 egg yolks, preferably free-range
1 tablesp. (1 American tablesp. + 1 teasp.) freshly chopped chives
   (optional)
salt and freshly ground pepper

seasoned white flour, preferably unbleached
beaten egg
fine dried breadcrumbs

Put the cold milk into a saucepan with the carrot, onion and herbs,
bring slowly to the boil, simmer for 3 or 4 minutes, turn off the heat and
allow to infuse for about 10 minutes if you have enough time. Strain the
flavourings, rinse them and add to a stock if you have one on the go.
Bring the milk back to the boil, whisk in the roux bit by bit; it will get
very thick but persevere. (The roux always seems like a lot too much
but you need it all so don't decide to use less.)

Season with salt and freshly ground pepper. Cook for 1–2 minutes on a
gentle heat, then remove from the heat, stir in the egg yolks, cheese and
optional chives. Taste and correct the seasoning. Spread out on a wide
plate to cool.

When the mixture is cold or at least cool enough to handle, shape into
balls about the size of a golf ball or 1 oz (30 g) approx. Roll first in
seasoned flour, then in beaten egg and then in fine breadcrumbs. Chill
until firm but bring back to room temperature before cooking otherwise
they may burst. Just before serving, heat a deep fryer to 150°C/300°F
and cook the Cheese Croquettes until crisp and golden. Drain on
kitchen paper and serve hot with a green salad and perhaps some
Ballymaloe Country Relish.

Note: Cooked Cheese Croquettes can be kept warm in an oven for up to
30 minutes. They can also be frozen and reheated in an oven.

*Pancakes

For family cooking you always need to have a few things up your sleeve that can be knocked up quickly in an emergency, and pancakes have always been one of my great standbys. If you arrive home late and everyone is starving you can whizz up some batter and within a few minutes the pancakes will be coming off the pan. Pancakes can be served in so many different ways, both sweet and savoury, that I call them the 'great convertibles'. They can be eaten straight off the pan, or stuffed and rolled, or shaped into little almspurses, or built in a pyramid, but surely the ultimate is the Crêpe Soufflée that John Desmond serves at his restaurant on Hare Island off Baltimore in West Cork. I have included it in the Puddings section.

ᵛ*Savoury Pancake Batter

Makes 12–18 depending on size of pan. An 11-inch (28 cm) pan makes 12 pancakes.

> 6 ozs (170 g/generous 1 cup) white flour, preferably unbleached
> good pinch of salt
> 2 large eggs and 1 *or* 2 egg yolks, preferably free-range
> scant ¾ pint (450 ml) milk, *or* for very crisp, light delicate pancakes, milk and water mixed
> 3–4 dessertsp. melted butter

Sieve the flour and salt into a bowl, make a well in the centre and drop in the lightly beaten eggs. With a whisk or wooden spoon, starting in the centre, mix the egg and gradually bring in the flour. Add the liquid slowly and beat until the batter is covered with bubbles.

Let the batter stand in a cold place for an hour or so — longer will do no harm. Just before you cook the pancakes stir in the melted butter. This will make all the difference to the flavour and texture of the pancakes and will make it possible to cook them without greasing the pan each time.

ᵛ*Herb Pancakes

Add to the batter 2 tablesp. (2 American tablesp. + 2 teasp.) freshly chopped herbs, e.g. parsley, thyme and chives and cook in the usual way.

To cook: Heat a heavy cast-iron crêpe pan or a non-stick pan to very hot, pour in just enough batter to cover the base of the pan thinly (a small ladle can also be useful for this), loosen the pancake around the edge, flip over with a spatula or thin egg slice, cook for a second or two on the other side and slide off the pan on to a plate. The pancakes may be stacked on top of each other and peeled apart later.

They will keep in the fridge for several days and also freeze perfectly. If they are to be frozen it's probably a good idea to put a disc of silicone paper between each for extra safety.

Note: If you have several pans it is perfectly possible to keep 3 or 4 pans going in rotation. But only necessary if you need to feed the multitudes!

ᵛ*Almspurses with Tomato Sauce

This is a fun way to serve a savoury pancake. Serve one as a starter or three each with a different filling for a substantial main course. The filling can include meat, fish or just a juicy vegetable filling.

>   **Savoury *or* Herb pancakes (see opposite), cooked on a 10-inch (25.5 cm) pan**
>
>   *Suggested Fillings*
>   ᵛ **Piperonata (see p. 69)**
>   ᵛ **Mushroom à la Crème (see p. 16)**
>   ᵛ **Tomato Fondue (see p. 68)**
>   ᵛ **Creamed Spinach**
>   **Seafood (see p. 48)**
>   **Chicken and Ham (see p. 49)**
>   **long chives for tying**
>   **Tomato Sauce (see below)**

To assemble: Lay a pancake on the worktop. Put a heaped dessertspoon of hot chosen filling into the centre. Gather the edges together and then tie into a purse shape with a blanched and refreshed chive. Serve on a hot plate surrounded by Tomato Sauce.

ᵛ*Tomato Sauce

Makes 16 fl ozs (475 ml/2 cups)

A good tomato sauce is a marvellous accompaniment to all sorts of dishes. I find it invaluable to have in the fridge or freezer as a standby. And of course you have a pasta sauce in seconds.

2 lbs (900 g) very ripe tomatoes, peeled and chopped *or* 2 x 14 oz
    (400 g) tins Italian tomatoes, chopped
1 oz (30 g/$\frac{1}{4}$ stick) butter
2 tablesp. (2 American tablesp. + 2 teasp.) extra virgin olive oil
1–4 cloves of garlic, depending on taste, peeled and chopped
1 medium onion, finely chopped
salt, freshly ground pepper and sugar

Melt the butter, add the olive oil and toss in the chopped garlic. Cook
for 1–2 minutes or until pale golden, then add the onion, cook for a
minute or two before adding the tomatoes, then season with salt, pepper
and sugar. Cook fast for 15–20 minutes if you want a fresh tasting sauce,
or more slowly — for up to 1 hour — if you prefer it more concentrated.
Purée through a mouli-légumes. Taste and correct the seasoning. Basil,
mint or annual marjoram could be added to the Tomato Sauce.

Note: One or two teaspoons of Balsamic vinegar stirred into the sauce
just before serving will intensify the flavour deliciously.

*Seafood Pancakes

Serves 4

Lots of other combinations would be delicious here. Remember to taste
your filling and serve it piping hot.

8 Savoury *or* Herb Pancakes (see p. 46) cooked on a 9-inch (23 cm)
    non-stick pan
1 x Mushroom à la Crème recipe (see p. 16)
16 prawns *or* shrimps
16 mussels steamed open and shells discarded *or* a mixture of
    cockles and mussels
4 ozs (110 g) cooked fish — salmon, monkfish, cod *or* grey sea mullet
a little freshly chopped parsley
salt and freshly ground pepper

Heat the Mushroom à la Crème, add the fish and stir carefully over a
gentle heat until the mixture has heated through. Add a little chopped
parsley, taste and correct the seasoning. If it is too thick add a little drop
of milk.

To assemble: Put one pancake on to a hot plate, spoon a quarter of the
filling into the centre, fold another pancake into a semi-circle and place

on top so that half the filling is exposed. Garnish with flat parsley and maybe a sprig of fennel.

Repeat with the other pancakes and serve immediately.

Variations
This is quite a simple version but one could spoon a sauce, e.g. a light Hollandaise, on top and glaze it under a grill for a few minutes. In fact if you have Hollandaise Sauce made, a spoonful stirred into the filling would make it even more delicious. This filling can also be used for Pancake Parcels or Almspurses.

*Chicken, Ham and Spring Onion Pancakes

Serves 4

> 4 large Savoury *or* Herb pancakes (see p. 46) — (I use 11 inch/28 cm but of course you can make them smaller if you wish.)
> 1 x Mushroom à la Crème recipe (see p. 16)
> 1 tablesp (1 American tablesp. + 1 teasp.) chopped spring onions (optional)
> 4 ozs (110 g) freshly cooked chicken
> 2 ozs (55 g) cooked ham *or* bacon
> a little milk (optional)

Heat the mushroom mixture and add the spring onions if using. Chop the chicken and ham into pieces about $\frac{3}{4}$ inch (2 cm), fold in gently. Add a little milk if it appears to be too thick. Allow to bubble until the mixture has heated through.

Put 2 tablespoons of the filling on to each pancake, fold in the edges and then roll them over to make a parcel. Proceed as below, reheat if necessary and serve piping hot with a tomato salad and a good green salad.

*Stuffed Pancakes, Pancake Parcels and variations

> Savoury *or* Herb pancakes (see p. 46)
>
> *Filling*
> Béchamel *or* Mornay Sauce (see pp 2 *or* 67)
> buttered crumbs (see p. 38)

Version 1
Lay a pancake on the work top, spoon 1–2 tablespoons of filling into the centre, fold in the sides to make a neat parcel. If the pancake and filling are hot, this can be eaten immediately with a sauce, e.g. a light Hollandaise or Tomato Sauce (see p. 47), otherwise cover and store in the fridge until needed.

To reheat: Transfer to a damp baking sheet and heat in a preheated moderate oven for 10–15 minutes. If you enjoy them crispy on top don't cover the baking sheet.

Version 2
Fill the pancake as above, preferably with a non-creamy filling. Shape into a neat parcel or a roll, arrange one or two in a buttered gratin dish, spoon over some Béchamel or Mornay Sauce, sprinkle with grated Cheddar cheese or a mixture of grated cheese and buttered crumbs.

Reheat in a moderate oven, 180°C/350°F/regulo 4, for 10–15 minutes or until hot and bubbly. If necessary flash under the grill for a few seconds before serving to brown and crisp the top.

Note: This method is particularly delicious for vegetarian pancakes filled with, e.g., Piperonata (see p. 69), Tomato Fondue (see p. 68) or a mixture of creamed spinach and sautéed mushrooms.

Version 3
Build up the pancakes in layers with one or several complementary fillings, spoon a sauce over the top and sprinkle with buttered crumbs or perhaps some chopped nuts. Reheat in a moderate oven, 180°C/350°F/regulo 4, and serve in slices like a piece of cake. This pancake 'gateau' can be either sweet or savoury.

Vegetarian Dishes

More and more people, teenagers in particular, are adopting a vegetarian way of life. For generations vegetarians were dismissed by arrogant meat-eaters as a bunch of 'nuts and flakes' who wore rope sandals and existed on a dreary diet of beans and lentils. Recently, however, with numbers growing at an astonishing rate (20 per cent per year in Britain) vegetarianism has taken on a new respectability. As a result many restaurants, and indeed schools, now offer a vegetarian menu.

Why such a dramatic increase? Well, the reasons are many and varied. More and more young people are deeply unhappy with what they consider to be the inhumane methods used in intensive farming nowadays. There is also a growing realisation that meat is not an essential component of a healthy diet. At the same time the range of vegetables, grains, pulses and fruit on offer in our shops becomes ever more tempting — coupled with a tantalising array of spices, fresh herbs and ethnic foods to liven up the vegetarian diet. Many families now enjoy vegetarian food once or twice a week even though they don't have a vegetarian member at all! We all love vegetarian food and enjoy the challenge of creating nutritious and delicious vegetarian recipes: the few included here, because of pressure on space, are just a taste. Many of the dishes in the Eggs, Cheese and Pancakes section will appeal to non-vegan vegetarians and are marked with the symbol ⱽ. Here and in the Vegetables section that follows I continue to use the ⱽ symbol for non-vegans, with ⱽⱽ indicating those dishes which are suitable for vegans.

ⱽ*A Warm Salad of Irish Goat's Cheese with Walnut Oil Dressing

Serves 4

This is a perfect supper dish. Include a few cherry tomatoes or a few strips of roast red pepper if you want it more substantial.

1 fresh soft Irish goat's cheese — Croghan, St Tola, Lough Caum, Cáis Chléire *or* St Macha (see p. 88)
a selection of lettuces and salad leaves — butterhead, frisée, oakleaf, radicchio trevisano, rocket, salad burnet and golden marjoram

12 slices toasted French bread
16–20 fresh walnut halves

Garnish
chive *or* **wild garlic flowers** *or* **marigold petals (*Calendula officinalis*
    — optional)**

Dressing
6 tablesp. (8 American tablesp.) extra virgin olive oil
    or **4 tablesp. (5 American tablesp.) walnut oil**
dash of Dijon mustard
2 tablesp. (2 American tablesp. + 2 teasp.) white wine vinegar
2 tablesp. (2 American tablesp. + 2 teasp.) sunflower *or* **arachide oil**

Wash and dry the salad leaves and tear the larger leaves into bite-sized bits. Make the Dressing by whisking all the ingredients together.

Cover each piece of toasted French bread with a $\frac{3}{4}$ inch (2 cm) slice of goat's cheese. Just before serving, preheat the grill. Place the slices of bread and cheese under the grill and toast for 5 or 6 minutes or until the cheese is soft and slightly golden.

Meanwhile, toss the salad greens lightly in just enough Dressing to make the leaves glisten; drop a small handful on to each plate. Place 1 or 3 hot goat's cheese croûtons on to each salad, scatter with a few walnut pieces and serve immediately. We sprinkle wild garlic, chive flowers or marigold flowers over the salad in season.

Note: This salad may be used either as a starter, main course or as a cheese course.

v vv *Black-eyed Beans with Mushrooms*

Serves 6

Beans are an almost perfect food, high in protein and without a scrap of fat or dreaded cholesterol. They are also cheap and highly versatile. Livened up with fresh herbs and spices they are certainly far from dull. This is high on my list of favourite vegetarian recipes. Essentially it is one of the many gems from Madhur Jaffrey's *A Taste of India* but I have adapted the recipe slightly. Fresh coriander makes a tremendous difference to the flavour. If you have any space buy a packet of seeds. It is really easy to grow, and even though you may find it an acquired taste at first you'll soon become addicted!

$\frac{1}{2}$ lb (225 g/scant 1$\frac{1}{4}$ cups) dried black-eyed beans
$\frac{1}{2}$ lb (225 g) fresh mushrooms
6 tablesp. (8 American tablesp.) sunflower *or* arachide oil
1 teasp. whole cumin seeds
1 inch (2.5 cm) piece of cinnamon stick
5 ozs (150 g/1 cup) onion, chopped
4 cloves of garlic, very finely chopped
14 ozs (400 g) fresh *or* tinned tomatoes, peeled and chopped
2 teasp. ground coriander seeds
1 teasp. ground cumin seeds
$\frac{1}{2}$ teasp. ground turmeric
pinch of sugar
$\frac{1}{4}$ teasp. cayenne pepper
1 good teasp. salt (it needs it, so don't cut down)
freshly ground black pepper
3 tablesp. (4 American tablesp.) freshly chopped coriander (fresh
  parsley may be substituted though the flavour is not at all the same)

Soak the beans in plenty of cold water overnight. Next day cover with fresh water, bring to the boil and simmer for 30 minutes approx. or until just cooked.

Cut the mushrooms into $\frac{1}{8}$ inch (3 mm) thick slices. Heat the oil in a sauté pan over a medium-high flame. When hot, put in the whole cumin seeds and the cinnamon stick. Let them sizzle for 5–6 seconds. Now put in the onions and garlic. Stir and fry until the onion is just beginning to colour at the edges. Put in the mushrooms. Stir and fry until the mushrooms wilt. Now put in the tomatoes, ground coriander, ground cumin, turmeric, pinch of sugar and cayenne. Stir and cook for a minute. Cover, and let this mixture cook on a gentle heat in its own juices for 10 minutes. Turn off the heat under the sauté pan. Drain the beans, reserving the cooking liquid, and add to the mushroom base mixture, add salt and freshly ground pepper, 2 tablespoons of the fresh coriander and $\frac{1}{4}$ pint (150 ml/generous $\frac{1}{2}$ cup) of bean cooking liquid.

Bring the beans to the boil again. Cover, reduce the heat and simmer for 20–30 minutes or until the beans are tender. Stir occasionally. Remove the cinnamon stick before serving. Sprinkle with the remaining tablespoon (1 American tablesp. + 1 teasp.) of fresh coriander.

^{v vv} *Chick Peas with Fresh Spices*

Serves 8–10

A few little jars of fresh spices are really a must for your store cupboard. They will add terrific zest and an exotic flavour to your food — especially if you are a vegetarian.

> 1 lb (450 g) chick peas (cover and soak overnight in cold water)
> 2 fresh green chillies
> 2-inch (5 cm) piece of fresh ginger, peeled and roughly chopped
> 4 cloves of garlic
> 4 tablesp. (5 American tablesp.) olive oil
> 8 ozs (225 g/1½ cups) onions, finely chopped
> 1 teasp. whole cumin seeds, crushed
> 2 teasp. whole coriander seeds, crushed
> 1–2 teasp. chilli powder
> 8 very ripe tomatoes, peeled and chopped
> salt and freshly ground pepper
> 2 tablesp. (2 American tablesp. + 2 teasp.) freshly chopped
>   coriander leaves
> 1 tablesp. (1 American tablesp. + 1 teasp.) fresh mint leaves

Drain the chick peas, cover with fresh water and cook until tender — this can take anything from 30–60 minutes depending on the quality. Drain and reserve the cooking liquid. Meanwhile remove the seeds from the chillies and grind to a paste in a pestle and mortar or food processor with the ginger and garlic.

Heat the oil in a heavy bottomed sauté pan, sweat the onions until soft but not coloured, add the chilli paste together with the crushed cumin, coriander seeds and the chilli powder. Cook for a minute or two, then add the peeled and chopped tomatoes, the drained chick peas and a little of the cooking liquid (save the rest for soup). Simmer gently for about 10 minutes until the flavours have mingled.

Taste and season with salt and freshly ground pepper. Sprinkle with freshly chopped coriander and mint and serve immediately. This is quite delicious served either hot or cold.

^{v vv} *Pasta*

A few packets of pasta are essential 'storm rations' for your store cupboard. How did we ever manage without them? I could write a book on pasta sauces alone but here are a few suggestions for some of our favourite 'quickies'. You'll know by now that we virtually always have Piperonata, Tomato Fondue and Mushroom à la Crème in the fridge, so if you have those you already have three different sauces and you can do endless further variations, e.g.

1 Piperonata or Tomato Fondue and crispy bacon
2 Tomato Fondue with cooked mussels, clams or a mixture
3 Mushroom à la Crème on its own with crispy bacon or tuna or cooked shellfish; add a little more milk to make it more saucy if necessary.

Apart from those the following three recipes are very quick and easy.

^{v vv} Spaghetti with Fresh Tomato Sauce

Serves 4

Note this foolproof way of cooking pasta *al dente!*

> **8 ozs (225 g) spaghetti**
>
> *Sauce*
> **4–6 tomatoes, seeded and diced**
> **4–6 tablesp. (5–8 American tablesp.) extra virgin olive oil**
> **1 clove of garlic, crushed**
> **salt and freshly ground pepper**
> **a good pinch of sugar**
> **1–2 tablesp. (1½–2½ American tablesp.) freshly chopped parsley, chives *or* basil *or* a mixture of these**

First cook the pasta. Bring a large pot of water to the boil and add salt. Put in the spaghetti and bring back to the boil. Cook for 2 minutes, then turn off the heat, cover the pot and let it sit for 10–15 minutes, depending on the thickness of the spaghetti. Strain immediately and toss in sauce.

To make this Fresh Tomato Sauce, heat the olive oil, add the tomato, garlic, seasonings, sugar and herbs and heat until barely warm. Serve with the pasta.

^{v vv} Pasta Olé, Olé, Olé

Serves 4

I created this really fast pasta sauce in shades of red, white and green, the colours of the Italian flag, in a rush of enthusiasm during the World Cup.

8 ozs (225 g) spaghetti
1 oz (30 g/$\frac{1}{4}$ stick) butter
2 tablesp. (2 American tablesp. + 2 teasp.) olive oil
1–2 red chillies
$\frac{1}{2}$ red pepper (2 ozs/55 g approx.) finely diced
4 spring onions (1 oz/30 g approx.) finely chopped
2 cloves of garlic, crushed
2 tablesp. (2 American tablesp. + 2 teasp.) finely chopped fresh parsley
2 ozs (55 g/$\frac{1}{2}$ cup) freshly grated Parmesan cheese (Parmigiano
   Reggiano is best; see also p. 88)

Cook the spaghetti *al dente* in the usual way (see p. 55). Meanwhile remove the seeds from the chilli and discard; chop the flesh finely. Melt the butter and oil, add the crushed garlic, onions, pepper dice and chillies and cook for 2 minutes. Drain the spaghetti, pour the sauce over it, sprinkle with parsley and toss well. Serve immediately with freshly grated Parmesan cheese.

v vv *Spaghetti with Olive Oil and Garlic*

Serves 6–8

1 lb (450 g) spaghetti *or* thin noodles

Sauce
2–3 ozs (55–85 g/$\frac{1}{2}$–$\frac{3}{4}$ stick) butter *or* $\frac{1}{2}$ butter and extra virgin olive oil
2 tablesp. (2 American tablesp. + 2 teasp.) freshly chopped parsley
1 tablesp. (1 American tablesp. + 1 teasp.) freshly chopped mint
2 tablesp. (2 American tablesp. + 2 teasp.) freshly chopped basil
2–4 large cloves of garlic, crushed
grated cheese — Parmesan *or* Irish Cheddar (see p. 88)

Cook the pasta until *al dente* in the usual way (see p. 55). Mix the herbs and crushed garlic with the olive oil or oil and butter. Sweat gently for 2 minutes, no longer. Stir into the hot spaghetti and serve with grated cheese — preferably Parmesan, though we often use Irish Cheddar.

v vv *Stir-fried Vegetables*

Serves 2–4

You can stir-fry a number of different vegetables but think about texture, colour and flavour before you make your choice. A wok is by far the most useful bit of kitchen equipment, but useless unless you have a powerful gas cooker. Having said that, a good heavy frying pan will suffice for this recipe.

2 tablesp. (2 American tablesp. + 2 teasp.) spring onions, cut into
    thin slices at an angle
1 tablesp. (1 American tablesp. + 1 teasp.) grated *or* finely chopped
    fresh ginger
2–3 cloves of garlic, chopped
2 ozs (55 g) mushrooms, cut into quarters and sliced thinly
$2\frac{1}{2}$ ozs (70 g) French beans, cut into $\frac{1}{4}$ inch (5 mm) thick slices at an
    angle
3 ozs (85 g) yellow *or* green courgettes, cut in half lengthways and
    sliced thinly
3 ozs (85 g) mangetout peas, cut into small pieces $\frac{1}{2}$ inch (1 cm)
    approx. at an angle
2 ozs (55 g) broccoli, cut into tiny florets
4–5 tablesp. (5–7 American tablesp.) olive oil
1 oz (30 g) peanuts *or* cashew nuts (optional)
salt and freshly ground pepper
pinch of sugar
1 tablesp. (1 American tablesp. + 1 teasp.) freshly chopped parsley
1 tablesp. (1 American tablesp. + 1 teasp.) freshly chopped mixed
    herbs — mint, chives, thyme *or* basil

1 tablesp. (1 American tablesp. + 1 teasp) oyster sauce (optional)
few drops of sesame oil (optional)

First prepare the vegetables. Heat the wok until it smokes, add the oil and heat again. Add the spring onions, ginger and garlic, toss around, then add the vegetables one after the other in the following order, tossing between each addition: mushrooms, French beans, courgettes, mangetout peas, broccoli and nuts. Season with salt, freshly ground pepper and sugar. Sprinkle with freshly chopped herbs, taste and correct the seasoning. Serve immediately in a hot serving dish.

If you would like your stir-fry to have an oriental flavour, add 1–2 tablespoons of oyster sauce or soy sauce instead of the herbs and sprinkle on a few drops of sesame oil just before serving.

Vegetables

If you glance at the contents list for this section you may wonder why it is entirely dominated by the humble spud! Well, now: despite the fact that potatoes are our best loved staple food we are incredibly unadventurous in our treatment of them. As many people just boil or mash them I have decided to include a whole array of dishes based on this healthy, nutritious and very inexpensive tuber.

Even though Ireland is famous the world over for its delicious, floury potatoes, there are many people in this country who would say: where on earth are they? If I had a penny for every time I have heard a complaint about how difficult it is to find really good potatoes, or for every time I have tried to explain the predicament of the potato growers, I would be a rich woman!

Basically, this is how I see it. Even though Irish potatoes are legendary we don't actually have an ideal climate in which to grow them; our warm, slightly wet summer weather is very conducive to blight. The varieties of potato which grow well in this country have an excellent flavour but are low-yielding. Since Ireland joined the EC, Irish potato growers have had to compete with cheaper imports from all over Europe. Their response has been to boost their yields with nitrogen, but the unfortunate consequence is loss of flavour, combined with poor keeping ability.

The potato farmers have now found themselves in a Catch 22 situation with many complaints from disgruntled customers. The simple fact of the matter is that if we want really good Irish potatoes that have not been boosted by nitrogen we are going to have to pay more. Already there are many farmers who are committed to producing better quality potatoes, so search for their produce and support them.

As soon as I heard that the EC in its wisdom had decided to limit the number of official potato varieties, I decided to plant some of the old varieties in the vegetable garden at Shanagarry. This year I grew eight different sorts, and we've had great fun cooking and tasting them.

I have, of course, included recipes for other vegetables — but not nearly as many as I would have liked because of shortage of space. Some readers may wonder why I have taken up some of my valuable space with the recipes for Tomato Fondue, Piperonata and Mushroom à la Crème, all of which have appeared in previous books. The answer is that they are all incredibly useful standbys in my own kitchen — so versatile that they pop up in a host of recipes which form the backbone of *Simply Delicious Food for Family & Friends*!

ᵛ*Gratin of Potato and Spring Onion

Serves 4 as a main course
Serves 6 as an accompaniment

Potato gratins are a tasty, nourishing and economical way to feed lots of hungry people on a chilly evening. This recipe could also include little pieces of bacon or a lamb chop cut into dice, so it can be a sustaining main course or a delicious accompaniment.

3 lbs (1.5 kg) 'old' potatoes — Golden Wonders *or* Kerr's Pinks
2 bunches of spring onions
1 oz (30 g/$\frac{1}{4}$ stick) butter
3–6 ozs (85–170 g/$\frac{3}{4}$ –1$\frac{1}{2}$ cups) Irish mature Cheddar cheese, grated
    (see p. 88)
salt and freshly ground pepper
$\frac{1}{2}$ –$\frac{3}{4}$ pint (300–450 ml/1$\frac{1}{4}$ –1$\frac{3}{4}$ cups) homemade chicken, beef *or*
    vegetable stock

I use an oval ovenproof gratin dish, 12$\frac{1}{2}$ inches (31.5 cm) x 2 inches (5 cm) deep.

Preheat the oven to 200°C/400°F/regulo 6.

Slice the potatoes thinly, blanch and refresh. Trim the spring onions and chop both the green and white parts into $\frac{1}{4}$ inch (5 mm) slices approx. with scissors or a knife.

Rub an ovenproof dish thickly with half the butter, scatter with some of the spring onions, then a layer of potatoes and some grated cheese. Season well with salt and freshly ground pepper. Continue to build up the layers, finishing with an overlapping layer of potatoes neatly arranged. Pour in the boiling stock, scatter with the remaining cheese and dot with butter.

Bake in a preheated oven for 1–1$\frac{1}{4}$ hours or until the potatoes are tender and the top is brown and crispy.

Note: It may be necessary to cover the potatoes with a paper lid for the first half of the cooking.

ᵛ*Gratin of Potato and Mushrooms

Serves 4

If you have a few wild mushrooms, e.g. Chanterelle or field mushrooms, mix them with ordinary mushrooms for this gratin. If all you can find are flat mushrooms, all the better. One way or the other it will still be delectable.

> 1 lb (450 g) peeled 'old' potatoes — Golden Wonders *or* Kerr's Pinks
> $\frac{1}{2}$ lb (225 g/4 cups) mushrooms
> $\frac{1}{4}$ oz (8 g) butter
> 1 clove of garlic, finely chopped
> salt and freshly ground pepper
> $\frac{1}{2}$ pint (300 ml/1$\frac{1}{4}$ cups) light cream
> 3 tablesp. (4 American tablesp.) grated Parmesan (Parmigiano
>   Reggiano) *or* Irish mature Cheddar cheese (see p. 88)

I use a square ovenproof gratin dish, 10 inches (25.5 cm) x 8$\frac{1}{2}$ inches (21.5 cm).

Slice the mushrooms. Peel the potatoes and slice thinly. Blanch and refresh. Grease a shallow gratin dish generously with butter and sprinkle the garlic over it. Arrange half the potatoes in the bottom of the dish, season with salt and freshly ground pepper, and put in the mushrooms. Season again and finish off with a final layer of overlapping potatoes. Bring the cream almost to boiling point and pour over the potatoes. Sprinkle the cheese on top and bake for 1$\frac{1}{2}$ hours approx. at 180°C/350°F/regulo 4, until the gratin becomes crisp and golden brown with the cream bubbling up around the edges.

This gratin is terrifically good with a pangrilled lamb chop or a piece of steak.

*Gratin of Potato and Smoked Salmon

Serves 4–6

There are really two recipes in one here. The basic recipe is a particularly good version of the classic French potato dish Gratin Dauphinois which is delicious served with a simple roast or grill. Here we've added little strips of smoked salmon to make a favourite supper dish. Serve with a good green salad (see p. 70).

60

2 lbs (900 g) even-sized, peeled 'old' potatoes — Golden Wonders
or Kerr's Pinks
salt and freshly ground pepper
9 fl ozs (275 ml/generous 1 cup) milk
9 fl ozs (275 ml/generous 1 cup) double cream
1 small clove of garlic, peeled and crushed
freshly grated nutmeg
1 tablesp. (1 American tablesp. + 1 teasp.) freshly chopped parsley
1 tablesp. (1 American tablesp. + 1 teasp.) freshly chopped chives
4–6 ozs (110–170 g) smoked Irish salmon

4 small ovenproof gratin dishes with $4\frac{1}{2}$-inch (11.5 cm) bottom and
6-inch (15 cm) top

Peel the potatoes and slice them into very thin rounds $\frac{1}{8}$ inch (3 mm) thick. Do not wash them but dab them dry with a cloth. Spread them out on the worktop and season with salt and freshly ground pepper, mixing it in with your hands. Pour milk into a saucepan, add the potatoes and bring to the boil. Cover, reduce the heat and simmer gently for 10 minutes.

Add the cream, garlic and a generous grating of fresh nutmeg. Continue to simmer for 20 minutes, stirring occasionally so that the potatoes do not stick to the saucepan. Just as soon as the potatoes are cooked, put a layer into each of the 4 ovenproof gratin dishes, sprinkle each with some parsley and chives, add $1–1\frac{1}{2}$ ozs (30–45 g) smoked salmon to each, cut into $\frac{1}{4}$-inch (5 mm) strips, and cover with another layer of potato.*

Reheat in a bain marie in a preheated oven, 200°C/400°F/regulo 6, for 8–10 minutes or until they are bubbly and golden on top. Sprinkle with chopped parsley and chives.

*Can be prepared ahead to this point.

Gratin Dauphinois
Proceed as above but omit the smoked salmon, parsley and chives.

ᵛ*Baked Potatoes

Serves 6–8

8 large (8 ozs/225 g approx) 'old' potatoes — Golden Wonders *or*
Kerr's Pinks
sea salt and butter

Scrub the skins of the potatoes very well. Prick each potato 3 or 4 times and bake in a preheated oven, 200°C/400°F/regulo 6, for 1 hour approx. depending on the size. When cooked, serve immediately while skins are still crisp and make sure to eat the skins with lots of butter and sea salt — Simply Delicious!

Suggested Stuffing for Baked Potatoes
1 Garlic mayonnaise with tuna fish
2 Fromage Blanc (Jockey) with smoked salmon and chives
3 Garlic butter with chopped crispy rasher

v vv *Rustic Roast Potatoes

Serves 4–6

These are my children's favourite kind of roast spuds. They particularly love all the crusty skin.

> **6 large 'old' potatoes — Golden Wonders *or* Kerr's Pinks**
> **olive oil *or* beef dripping (unless for vegetarians)**
> **sea salt**

Preheat the oven to 230°C/450°F/regulo 8.

Scrub the potatoes well, cut into quarters lengthways or cut into rounds $\frac{3}{4}$ inch (2 cm). Put into a roasting tin, drizzle with olive oil and toss so they are barely coated with oil. Roast in the preheated oven for 15–20 minutes depending on size.

Sprinkle with sea salt and serve.

v vv Crusty Potatoes with Ginger and Garlic

Serves 4–5

In parts of India they eat almost as many potatoes as the Irish, but they don't just boil or roast them — many are deliciously spiced. This recipe which was given to me by Madhur Jaffrey is one of my favourites.

> **1$\frac{1}{2}$ lbs (675 g) 'old' potatoes — Golden Wonders *or* Kerr's Pinks**
> **piece of fresh ginger, about 2 x 1 x 1 inches (5 x 2.5 x 2.5 cm), peeled**
> **   and coarsely chopped**
> **3 cloves of garlic, peeled and crushed**
> **3 tablesp. (4 American tablesp.) water**
> **$\frac{1}{2}$ teasp. ground turmeric**

1 teasp. salt

$\frac{1}{2}$ teasp. cayenne pepper

5 tablesp. (7 American tablesp.) sunflower *or* peanut oil

1 teasp. whole fennel seeds (optional)

Boil the potatoes in their jackets until just cooked. Drain them and let them cool. Peel the potatoes and cut them into $\frac{3}{4}$–1 inch (2–2.5 cm) dice. Put the chopped fresh ginger, crushed garlic, water, turmeric, salt and cayenne pepper into the container of a food processor and blend to a paste.

Heat the oil in a large non-stick frying pan over a medium flame. When hot, put in the fennel seeds (if using). Let them sizzle for a few seconds (be careful not to let them burn) and add in the spice paste. Stir and fry for 2 minutes. Put in the potatoes. Stir and fry for 5–7 minutes over a medium-high flame or until the potatoes have a nice, golden-brown crust. Sprinkle with chopped parsley or coriander. Serve on their own, perhaps with Cucumber and Yoghurt Raita (see p. 25) or as an accompaniment to grilled or roast meat.

v *Potato Cakes

Serves 8

Called Potato Bread or Fadge in Ulster, this is just the thing to bring a light to an Ulsterman's eye. Although I'm not sure he'd approve of the herbs! Potato Cakes can be cooked on a baking sheet in the oven. Left-over mashed or Duchesse Potato (see *Simply Delicious 2*, p. 63) may also be used for them. They are delicious even with just a few crispy rashers.

2 lbs (900 g) unpeeled 'old' potatoes — Golden Wonders *or* Kerr's Pinks

1–2 eggs, preferably free-range

1–2 ozs (30–55 g/$\frac{1}{4}$ – $\frac{1}{2}$ stick) butter

2 tablesp. (2 American tablesp. + 2 teasp.) white flour, preferably unbleached

1 tablesp. (1 American tablesp. + 1 teasp.) freshly chopped mixed parsley, chives and lemon thyme (optional)

salt and freshly ground pepper

creamy milk

seasoned white flour, preferably unbleached

bacon fat, butter *or* olive oil for frying

Boil the potatoes in their jackets, pull off the peel and mash right away, adding the beaten eggs, butter, flour and herbs. Season with lots of salt and freshly ground pepper, adding a few drops of creamy milk if the mixture is too stiff. Taste and correct the seasoning. Shape the potato cakes into rounds about 3 inches (7.5 cm) in diameter and scant 1 inch (2.5 cm) thick. Dip in seasoned flour.

Melt some bacon fat, butter or olive oil in a frying pan on a gentle heat. Fry the potato cakes until golden on one side, then flip over and cook on the other side, 4–5 minutes approx. total cooking time. They should be crusty and golden. Serve on hot plates.

v vv *The Perfect Chip

Sales of frozen and prepared chips have rocketed in a relatively short time, so much that I feel many people have forgotten how easy it is to make chips at home.

The secret of really sensational chips is as follows:

1 Use really good quality 'old' potatoes, e.g. Golden Wonders or Kerr's Pinks.

2 Use best-quality oil, lard or beef fat for frying. I frequently use olive oil because its flavour is so good and because when properly looked after it can be used over and over again. Avoid poor quality oils which have an unpleasant taste and a pervasive smell.

3 Scrub the potatoes and peel or leave unpeeled according to taste. Cut into similar size chips so they will cook evenly.

4 Rinse the chips quickly in cold water but do not soak; dry them meticulously with a damp tea towel or kitchen towel before cooking.

You could make:

Straw Potatoes — finest possible strips about $2\frac{1}{2}$ inches (6.5 cm) long
Matchstick — similar length but slightly thicker
Mignonette — $\frac{1}{4}$ inch (5 mm) thick by $2\frac{1}{2}$ inches (6.5 cm) long
Pont Neuf — about $\frac{1}{2}$ inch (1 cm) thick and $2\frac{1}{2}$ inches (6.5 cm) long
Jumbo Chips — $\frac{3}{4}$ inches (2 cm) thick and $2\frac{1}{2}$ inches (6.5 cm) long
Buffalo Chips — similar size to Jumbo but unpeeled

To cook the first three types: Fry quickly in oil at 195°C/385°C until completely crisp.

To cook the last three sizes: Fry twice, once at 160°C/320°F until they are soft and just beginning to brown (the time will vary from 4–10 minutes

Black-eyed Beans with Mushrooms

Stir-fried Vegetables

Gratin of Potato and Spring Onion

Chocolate Fudge Pudding

Caramelised Honey and Almond Tart

Crêpes with Orange Butter

depending on size) then drain, increase the heat to 190°C/375°F and cook for a further 1–2 minutes or until crisp and golden. Shake the basket, drain well, toss on to kitchen paper, sprinkle with a little salt, turn on to a hot serving dish and serve immediately.

ᵛ ᵛᵛ *Potato Crisps or Game Chips*

These are paper-thin rounds of potato which are fried at 180°C/350°F until absolutely crisp. Drain on kitchen paper and sprinkle with salt. Serve hot or cold.

Provided they are properly cooked they will keep perfectly in a tin box for several days. These crisps or game chips are the traditional accompaniment to roast pheasant or guinea fowl.

ᵛ ᵛᵛ *Garlic Crisps*

Cook the crisps as above. Put them into a hot serving dish, melt some garlic butter and drizzle it over the crisps. Serve immediately as a snack or as an accompaniment to hamburgers or steaks or on a salade tiède.

ᵛ*Potato Salad

Serves 4–6

The secret of really good Potato Salad is to dress the potatoes while they are still warm.

> 2 lbs (900 g) freshly cooked potatoes, diced (allow about 2¼ lbs/1.1 kg
>   raw potatoes) — Pink Fir Apple, Sharpes Express *or* Golden
>   Wonders
> 1 tablesp. (1 American tablesp. + 1 teasp.) freshly chopped parsley
> 1 tablesp. (1 American tablesp. + 1 teasp.) freshly chopped chives *or*
>   scallions
> 4 fl ozs (120 ml/½ cup) French Dressing (see *Simply Delicious*, p. 57)
> ¼ cup homemade mayonnaise (optional — see *Simply Delicious 2*, p. 15)
> salt and freshly ground pepper

The potatoes should be boiled in their jackets then peeled, diced and measured while still hot. Mix immediately with the parsley and chives or scallions. Season well with salt and freshly ground pepper. Stir in the French dressing, allow to cool and finally add the homemade mayonnaise if using. Keeps well for about 2 days.

ᵛ ᵛᵛ *Roast Onions

I'm always surprised that so few people cook onions in this ultra simple way. We call them Roast Onions but I suppose strictly speaking they are baked. One way or the other they are absolutely delicious and my children adore them. Choose small or medium-sized onions. Preheat the oven to 200°C/400°F/regulo 6. Cook the unpeeled onions on a baking tray until soft; this can take anything from 10 to 30 minutes depending on size. Serve in their jackets. To eat, cut off the root end, squeeze out the onion and enjoy with butter and sea salt.

ᵛ ᵛᵛ *Roast Parsnips

Serves 6–8

My children love Roast Parsnips and ask for them three or four times a week during the parsnip season. Don't buy them washed, as they may have been treated with a bleach to keep them white.

> **4 parsnips**
> **beef dripping** *or* **olive oil**

Peel the parsnips and cut them into quarters (the chunks should be quite large). Blanch, refresh and dry well. Parsnips may also be cooked unblanched. Put them around a roast so that they become soft and golden brown in the juices and fat of the meat. Alternatively, you could roast parsnips on their own in beef dripping or olive oil in a hot oven, 230°C/450°F/regulo 8. We often roast them in the same pan as Rustic Roast Potatoes (see p. 62). Cooked this way they will be crisp outside; turn them frequently so that they do not become too crusty.

ᵛ Glazed Carrots

Serves 4–6

Despite the fact that carrots are our most common vegetable, they are rarely well cooked, often tasting watery and dull. They are best cooked in very little water. You might like to try this method which undoubtedly takes a little vigilance but the result is a revelation to many. Always buy carrots unwashed; they will have more flavour and keep better.

> **1 lb (450 g) carrots — Early Nantes and Autumn King have**
> **particularly good flavour**
> **$\frac{3}{4}$ oz (20 g/scant $\frac{1}{4}$ stick) butter**

4 fl ozs (100 ml/$\frac{1}{2}$ cup) cold water
pinch of salt
good pinch of sugar

Garnish
freshly chopped parsley *or* **fresh mint**

Cut off the tops and tips, scrub and peel thinly if necessary. Cut into slices $\frac{1}{3}$ inch (7 mm) thick, either straight across or at an angle. Leave very young carrots whole. Put them in a saucepan with the butter, water, salt and sugar. Bring to the boil, cover and cook over a gentle heat until tender, by which time all the liquid should have been absorbed into the carrots, but if not remove the lid and increase the heat until all the water has evaporated. Taste and correct the seasoning. Shake the saucepan so the carrots become coated with the buttery glaze. Serve in a hot vegetable dish sprinkled with chopped parsley or mint.

^v *Cauliflower Cheese*

Serves 6–8

I have rather despaired of cauliflower, having failed to find the name of the old variety which we ate as children. Cauliflower varieties seem to have suffered more from the point of view of flavour than most other vegetables. The leaves have more flavour than the curd so make sure not to discard them. Even a mediocre cauliflower can be made to taste delicious in a bubbling cheese sauce.

1 medium-sized cauliflower with green leaves
salt

Mornay Sauce
4 ozs (110 g/1 cup) grated cheese — Cheddar *or* **a mixture of**
    Gruyère, Parmesan and Cheddar
1 pint (600 ml/2$\frac{1}{2}$ cups) Béchamel sauce (see p. 2)
$\frac{1}{4}$ teasp. Dijon mustard
salt and freshly ground pepper

1 oz (30 g/$\frac{1}{4}$ cup) grated mature Cheddar cheese for the top (see p. 88)
freshly chopped parsley

Remove the outer leaves and wash both the cauliflower and the leaves well. Put not more than 1 inch (2.5 cm) water in a saucepan just large enough to take the cauliflower; add a little salt. Chop the leaves into

67

small pieces and either leave the cauliflower whole or cut in quarters; place the cauliflower on top of the green leaves in the saucepan, cover and simmer until cooked, 15 minutes approx. Test by piercing the stalk with a knife: there should be just a little resistance. Remove the cauliflower and leaves to an ovenproof serving dish.

Meanwhile make the Mornay sauce. Make the Béchamel sauce in the usual way and at the end add the 4 ozs (110 g/1 cup) grated cheese and a little mustard. Season with salt and freshly ground pepper, taste and correct the seasoning if necessary. Spoon the sauce over the cauliflower and sprinkle with the 1 oz grated cheese.*

Put into a hot oven, 230°C/450°F/regulo 8, or under the grill to brown. If the Cauliflower Cheese is allowed to get completely cold, it will take 20–25 minutes to reheat in a moderate oven, 180°C/350°F/regulo 4.

Serve sprinkled with freshly chopped parsley.

Note: If the cauliflower is left whole, cut a deep cross in the stalk.

* The dish may be prepared ahead to this point.

ᵛLeeks Mornay
Top and tail medium-sized leeks. Cook in a little boiling salted water until tender, drain and proceed as above.

Ham and Leek Mornay
Proceed as above but wrap each leek in a slice of cooked ham before coating with the cheese sauce, then continue as above.

ᵛ ᵛᵛ Tomato Fondue

Serves 6 approx.

This wonderful tomato stew, literally 'melted tomatoes', is best made during the summer months when the tomatoes are very ripe, but it can still be very good made with tinned tomatoes in winter. It is another of my 'great convertibles': we serve it not only as a vegetable but also as a sauce, a filling for pancakes and omelettes or a topping for pizzas. Reduce it a little more for pizza topping or it may be too sloppy.

> **2 lbs (900 g) very ripe tomatoes** *or* $\frac{1}{2}$ **fresh and** $\frac{1}{2}$ **tinned**
> **4 ozs (110 g/1 cup) sliced onions**
> **1 clove of garlic, crushed (optional)**
> **1 dessertsp. olive oil**

1 tablesp. (1 American tablesp. + 1 teasp.) of any of the following,
   freshly chopped: thyme, parsley, mint, basil, lemon balm *or*
   marjoram
salt, freshly ground pepper and sugar

Sweat the sliced onions and garlic (if used) in oil on a gentle heat. It is
vital for the success of this dish that the onions are completely soft
before the tomatoes are added. Remove the hard core from the
tomatoes. Put them into a deep bowl and cover them with boiling
water. Count to 10 and then pour off the water immediately; peel off the
skins, slice and add to the onions. Season with salt, freshly ground
pepper and sugar and add a generous sprinkling of chopped herb.
Cook for just 10–20 minutes more, or until the tomato softens.

Tomato Fondue will keep well in the fridge for up to 5 days.

ᵛ ᵛᵛ *Piperonata*

Serves 8–10

This is one of the indispensable trio of vegetable stews that we always
make a point of having to hand. We use it not only as a vegetable but
also as a topping for pizzas, a sauce for pasta, grilled fish or meat and
as a filling for omelettes and pancakes.

    2 red peppers
    2 green peppers
    1 onion, sliced
    6 large tomatoes (dark red and very ripe)
    2 tablesp. (2 American tablesp. + 2 teasp.) olive oil
    1 clove of garlic, crushed
    salt, freshly ground pepper and sugar
    few leaves of fresh basil

Heat the olive oil in a casserole, add the garlic and cook for a few
seconds, then add the sliced onion, toss in the oil and allow to soften
over a gentle heat in a covered casserole while the peppers are being
prepared. Halve the peppers, remove the seeds carefully, cut into
quarters and then into strips across rather than lengthways. Add to the
onion and toss in the oil; replace the lid and continue to cook.

Meanwhile peel the tomatoes (scald in boiling water for 10 seconds,
pour off the water and peel immediately). Slice the tomatoes and add
them to the casserole. Season with salt, freshly ground pepper, sugar

and a few leaves of fresh basil if available. Cook until the vegetables are just soft, 30 minutes approx.

Piperonata will keep well in the fridge for up to 5 days.

ᵛ ᵛᵛ *Kinoith Summer Garden Salad*

> **a selection of fresh lettuces and salad leaves — butterhead, oakleaf, iceberg, saladisi, mysticana, lollo rosso, frisée, radicchio, red orah leaves, rocket (Arugula), edible chrysanthemum leaves, wild sorrel leaves *or* buckler leaf sorrel, golden marjoram, salad burnet, borage, nasturtium flowers, marigold petals, chive *or* wild garlic flowers, herb leaves — lemon balm, mint, flat parsley**

Cider Vinegar Dressing
6 fl ozs (175 ml/$\frac{3}{4}$ cup) extra virgin olive oil
2 fl ozs (50 ml) cider vinegar
2 teasp. Lakeshore mustard with honey *or* Moutarde de Meaux
1 small clove of garlic, crushed
$\frac{1}{2}$ teasp. pure Irish honey
salt and freshly ground pepper

First make the dressing. Mix all the ingredients together, perhaps in a jam jar, shake and whisk well before use.

Wash and dry the lettuces and salad leaves, and tear into bite-sized bits. Sprinkle with edible flowers and petals. Just before serving toss in a little dressing — not too much, just enough to coat the leaves lightly. Serve immediately.

This makes almost $\frac{1}{2}$ pint (300 ml/$1\frac{1}{4}$ cups) of dressing so you will have enough for several salads. Store in a covered jar in a cool place (but not a fridge because the olive oil would solidify).

Puddings

In the crazy, diet-conscious times in which we live, few people allow themselves the luxury of a pudding every day — but few of us can resist the temptation of a luscious dessert now and again, and sure why not!

Meringue confections and ice cream extravaganzas are all very well, but apple tarts of some kind seem to come out on top as the all-time favourite, so I feel it is impossible to have too many good recipes. The Cullohill Apple Pie is a real gem because the pastry can be made without the slightest difficulty, even by an eight-year-old.

There are lots of other old favourites here too, including an irresistible Chocolate Fudge Pudding, an easy Vanilla Ice Cream (another great freezer standby), Apple Crumble and a Bread and Butter Pudding that will earn you a standing ovation from the family even if you are only using up the crusts!

ᵛ Chocolate Fudge Pudding

Serves 6–8

Chocolate puddings run neck-and-neck with apple tarts as most people's favourite dessert. This one is wickedly rich with a melting texture. It should be moist in the centre, so don't overcook or it will be dull. It is also good cold.

>   5 ozs (140 g) best quality chocolate
>   5 ozs (140 g/1¼ sticks) butter
>   1 teasp. pure vanilla essence
>   ¼ pint (150 ml/generous ½ cup) warm water
>   4 ozs (110 g/generous ½ cup) castor sugar
>   4 eggs, preferably free-range
>   1 oz (30 g/scant ¼ cup) self-raising white flour, preferably
>   unbleached
>
>   pie dish, 2 pint (1.1 L/5 cup) capacity, well greased with a little
>   butter, *or* 7 individual 3-inch (7.5 cm) ramekins

Preheat the oven to 200°C/400°F/regulo 6.

Cut up the chocolate into small pieces and melt with the butter in a very low oven or in a pyrex bowl over simmering water. As soon as the chocolate has melted, remove from the heat and add the vanilla essence, then stir in the warm water and the castor sugar. Continue to mix until the mixture is smooth. Separate the eggs, whisk the yolks into the chocolate mixture, then fold in the sieved flour, making sure there are no lumps. Whisk the egg whites in a clean bowl until it reaches stiff peaks; fold gently into the chocolate mixture and pour into the greased pie dish.

Put the pie dish into a bain marie of hot water and bake in the preheated oven for 10 minutes, then lower the heat to 160°C/325°F/ regulo 3 for a further 20–30 minutes.* It should be firm on top but still soft and fudgy underneath. Serve hot or cold with softly whipped cream.

*Individual dishes take 15 minutes approx. at 200°C/400°F/regulo 6.

ᵛ*Bread and Butter Pudding

Serves 6–8

Bread and Butter Pudding is an irresistible way of using up left-over white bread. This is a particularly delicious recipe which causes a sensation every time we make it.

12 slices good-quality white bread, crusts removed
2 ozs (55 g/$\frac{1}{2}$ stick) butter, preferably unsalted
$\frac{1}{2}$ teasp. freshly grated nutmeg *or* cinnamon *or* mixed spice
7 ozs (200 g/1$\frac{1}{4}$ cups) plump raisins *or* sultanas
4 large eggs, preferably free-range, beaten lightly
8 fl ozs (225 ml/1 cup) milk
16 fl ozs (475 ml/2 cups) cream
1 teasp. pure vanilla essence
6 ozs (170 g/$\frac{3}{4}$ cup) castor sugar
pinch of salt
1 tablesp. (1 American tablesp. + 1 teasp.) granulated sugar for
    sprinkling on top

Garnish
softly whipped cream

pottery *or* china dish, 8 inches (20.5 cm) square

72

Butter the bread and arrange 4 slices, butter side down, in a single layer in the dish. Sprinkle the bread with half the nutmeg and half the raisins, arrange another layer of bread, buttered side down over the raisins and sprinkle the remaining nutmeg and raisins on top. Cover with the remaining bread, buttered side down.

In a bowl whisk together the eggs, milk, cream, vanilla essence, sugar and salt. Pour the mixture through a fine sieve over the bread. Sprinkle the granulated sugar over the top and let the mixture stand, covered loosely, at room temperature for at least 1 hour or chill overnight.

Bake in a bain marie — the water should be half way up the sides of the baking dish. Bake the pudding in the middle of the preheated oven, 180°C/350°F/regulo 4, for 1 hour approx. or until the top is crisp and golden. Serve the pudding warm with some softly whipped cream.

Note: This pudding reheats perfectly.

^v*Cullohill Apple Pie

Serves 8–12

Patrons of my family's pub, the Sportsman's Inn in Cullohill, Co. Laois will be familiar with this apple tart. The pastry is made by the creaming method so people who are convinced that they suffer from 'hot hands' don't have to worry about rubbing in the butter.

Pastry
8 ozs (225 g/2 sticks) butter
2 ozs (55 g/$\frac{1}{3}$ cup) castor sugar
2 eggs, preferably free-range
12 ozs (340 g/2$\frac{1}{2}$ cups) white flour, preferably unbleached

Filling
1$\frac{1}{2}$ lbs (675 g) Bramley Seedling cooking apples
5 ozs (140 g/$\frac{2}{3}$ cup) sugar
2–3 cloves

castor sugar for sprinkling

To serve
softly whipped cream
Barbados sugar

tin, 7 inches (18 cm) x 12 inches (30.5 cm) x 1 inch (2.5 cm) deep

Preheat the oven to 180°C/350°F/regulo 4.

First make the pastry. Cream the butter and sugar together by hand or in a food mixer. Add the eggs and beat for several minutes. Reduce speed and mix in the flour. This pastry needs to be chilled for at least 1 hour otherwise it is difficult to handle.

To make the tart: Roll out the pastry $\frac{1}{8}$ inch (3 mm) thick approx. and use about two-thirds of it to line a suitable tin. Peel, quarter and slice the apples into the tart, sprinkle with sugar and add the cloves. Cover with a lid of pastry, seal the edges, decorate with pastry leaves, egg wash and bake in the preheated oven until the apples are tender, approx. 45 minutes to 1 hour. When cooked cut into squares, sprinkle lightly with castor sugar and serve with softly whipped cream and Barbados sugar.

^v *Rhubarb Tart*

Make in exactly the same way but use 16 ozs (450 g) approx. finely chopped red rhubarb and approx. $6\frac{1}{2}$–7 ozs (185–200 g) sugar.

Alternative suggestions

^v Rhubarb and Strawberry

^v Apple and Mincemeat

^v Apple and Raspberry

^v Apple and Mixed Spice

^v Apple, Sultanas and Cinnamon

^v Green Gooseberry and Elderflower

^v Worcesterberry

^v Plum

^v Damson

^v *Dutch Apple Cake*

Serves 10–12 approx.

Another good apple pudding which we cook in a roasting tin. The recipe can be adapted for other fruit, e.g. apricots, peaches or plums.

> 3–4 Bramley Seedling cooking apples
> 2 large eggs, preferably free-range
> 8 ozs (225 g/1 generous cup) castor sugar
> 4 ozs (110 g/1 stick) butter
> $\frac{1}{4}$ pint (150 ml/generous $\frac{1}{2}$ cup) creamy milk
> $6\frac{1}{2}$ ozs (185 g) plain white flour, preferably unbleached

3 teasp. baking powder
1 oz (30 g) sugar

roasting tin, 8 inches (20.5 cm) x 12 inches (30.5 cm)
 or **lasagne dish, 10½ inches (26.5 cm) x 6½ inches (15 cm)**

Preheat the oven to 200°C/400°F/regulo 6.

Grease and flour the roasting tin. Whisk the eggs and castor sugar together until the mixture is thick and fluffy and the whisk leaves a figure of 8. Put the butter and milk into a saucepan, bring to the boil and whisk at once into the eggs and sugar. Sieve the flour and baking powder together and fold carefully into the batter so that there are no lumps. Pour the mixture into the prepared roasting tin.

Peel and core the apples, cut into thin slices and arrange them over the batter. Sprinkle with the remaining sugar. Bake in the preheated oven for 10 minutes, then reduce the heat to 180°C/350°F/regulo 4, for a further 20–25 minutes or until well risen and golden brown. Cool in the tin, then cut into slices. Serve with softly whipped cream.

^v *Apple Crumble*

Serves 6–8

Another very simple pudding that finds great favour chez moi.

1½ lbs (675 g) Bramley Seedling cooking apples
1½ –2 ozs (45–55 g) sugar
1–2 tablesp. (1½ –2½ American tablesp.) water

Crumble
4 ozs (110 g) white flour, preferably unbleached
2 ozs (55 g/½ stick) butter
2 ozs (55 g) castor sugar

pie dish, 2 pint (1.1 L) capacity

Stew the apples gently with the sugar and water in a covered casserole or stainless steel saucepan until about half cooked. Taste and add more sugar if necessary. Turn into a pie dish. Allow to cool slightly while you make the crumble.

Rub the butter into the flour just until the mixture resembles coarse bread crumbs, then add the sugar. Sprinkle this mixture over the apple in the pie dish. Bake in a preheated moderate oven 180°C/350°F/regulo 4, for

30–45 minutes or until the topping is cooked and golden. Serve with whipped cream and soft brown sugar.

^v*Blackberry and Apple Crumble*
Stew together three-quarters apple to one-quarter fresh or frozen black-berries and proceed as above.

^v*Rhubarb*
Stew rhubarb with sugar until almost cooked and proceed as above.

^v*Rhubarb and Strawberry*
Stew two-thirds rhubarb with sugar, stir in one-third strawberries and proceed as above.

^v*Gooseberry*
Stew green gooseberries with brown sugar and proceed as above.

^v*Gooseberry and Elderflower*
Stew green gooseberries with white sugar, add 2 elderflower heads tied in muslin while stewing, remove the elderflowers and proceed as above.

^v*Plum or Apricot*
Stew the plums or apricots as above.

^v*Variations on the Topping*
1 1 oz (30 g) oatflakes or sliced hazelnuts or nibbed almonds could also be added to the crumble.

2 1 teaspoonful of ground cinnamon or mixed spice is also a delicious addition.

^v*Caramelised Honey and Almond Tart*

Serves 8–10

I was so taken by my visit to Kevin Walker, a beekeeper who lives at Carrigeen, Kilglass, Co. Roscommon, that I have now got some bees myself. I'm not sure I'll ever make a natural beekeeper but it's worth every ounce of effort for the wonderful honey that the bees make from the blossoms in our orchard and gardens.

Pastry
6 ozs (170 g/generous 1 cup) white flour, preferably unbleached
1 oz (30 g) castor sugar

4 ozs (110 g/1 stick) butter
1 egg yolk, preferably free-range
drop of pure vanilla essence

Filling
1 tablesp. (1 American tablesp. + 1 teasp.) pure Irish honey
6 ozs (170 g) flaked almonds
3 ozs (85 g/$\frac{3}{4}$ stick) butter
1$\frac{1}{2}$ ozs (45 g) light brown sugar
1 tablesp. (1 American tablesp. + 1 teasp.) cream

round tin with a pop up bottom, 10-inch (25.5 cm) diameter

Put the flour and castor sugar into a bowl, rub in the butter and bind with the egg yolk and the vanilla essence. This is a tricky pastry to handle so if you like just press it into the greased tin. Prick the pastry, line it with kitchen paper and dried beans and bake in a preheated oven at 180°C/350°F/regulo 4, for 15–18 minutes or until pale golden.

To make the filing, put the butter, sugar, honey and almonds into a saucepan and cook over a low heat until they are pale straw colour; add the cream and cook for a few more seconds. Spread this mixture over the base and bake until the topping is a deep golden brown colour.* Cool on a wire rack. Serve with softly whipped cream.

*This can take anything from 8–20 minutes depending on the length of time the original ingredients were cooked.

ᵛ*John Desmond's Crêpe Soufflée

Serves 8

Makes 15 pancakes

You certainly won't whip this up in a couple of minutes, but if you want to do something really special for your family or friends, this is the ultimate crêpe, made for us by John Desmond in his restaurant on Hare Island.

John Desmond works in gram measurements.

Crêpe Batter
3$\frac{3}{4}$ ozs (100 g/scant 1 cup) white flour, preferably unbleached
scant $\frac{1}{4}$ oz (5 g) sugar
scant $\frac{1}{4}$ oz (5 g) salt
2 eggs, preferably free-range

1 egg yolk, preferably free-range
9 fl ozs (250 g/1 generous cup) milk
$1\frac{3}{4}$ ozs (50 g/$\frac{1}{2}$ stick) melted butter

Lemon Curd
juice of 3 lemons
zest of 3 lemons
5 ozs (150 g/$\frac{3}{4}$ cup) sugar
$1\frac{3}{4}$ ozs (50 g/$\frac{1}{2}$ stick) butter
8 egg yolks, preferably free-range

12 egg whites, preferably free-range
$1\frac{3}{4}$ ozs (50 g) sugar

icing sugar for dusting

Caramel Sauce (see opposite)

cast-iron *or* non stick crêpe pan 6-inch (15 cm) diameter

Make the pancake batter in the usual way (see opposite) and strain. Cover and allow to rest in the fridge for 1 hour or more. Cook the pancakes.

Next make the Caramel Sauce (see opposite) and keep it aside while you make the lemon curd base for the soufflé.

Put the lemon juice, zest, sugar and butter into a stainless steel saucepan and bring to the boil. Whisk the egg yolks in a bowl, then pour the boiling mixture on to the egg yolks in a steady stream whisking all the time. Put everything back into the saucepan and stir over a gentle heat until the mixture thickens to coat the back of a spoon. Pour it back into the bowl and keep warm while you whip the egg whites.

Preheat the oven to 150°C/300°F/regulo 2.

Whisk the egg whites in a spotlessly clean bowl until firm, fold in the sugar and whisk very quickly for a few seconds. Stir one-quarter of the egg mixture into the lemon curd and then gently but firmly fold in the rest. Put a large spoonful, the equivalent of about 2 heaped tablespoons of the soufflé mixture on to each crêpe and fold over so that they are half moon shape.

Arrange them side by side on a buttered baking sheet and bake in the preheated oven for 7 minutes.

To serve: Pour a little of the Caramel Sauce on each warm plate, dust the crêpes with icing sugar, place one on each plate and serve immediately — Simply Exquisite!

Caramel Sauce

7 ozs (200 g/1 cup) sugar
4 fl ozs (100 ml/$\frac{1}{2}$ cup) water
1$\frac{3}{4}$ ozs (50 g/$\frac{1}{2}$ stick) butter
juice of 1 orange
juice of 2 lemons

Put the sugar and water into a heavy bottomed saucepan. Stir until all the sugar has dissolved, then remove the spoon and continue to simmer until the syrup caramelises to a chestnut colour. Add the orange and lemon juice, stir and simmer for 2–3 minutes, swirl in the butter and serve.

^{v}*Crêpes with Orange Butter

Serves 6 — makes 12 approx.

This crêpe recipe is very nearly as good as those Crêpes Suzette they used to serve with a great flourish in posh restaurants when I was a child. These are only half the bother and can be made for a fraction of the cost.

Pancake Batter
6 ozs (170 g/generous 1 cup) white flour, preferably unbleached
good pinch of salt
1 dessertsp. (2 American teasp.) castor sugar
2 large eggs and 1 *or* 2 egg yolks, preferably free-range
scant $\frac{3}{4}$ pint (450 ml) milk — for very crisp, light delicate pancakes,
    use milk and water mixed
3–4 dessertsp. melted butter

Orange Butter
3 teasp. finely grated orange rind
6 ozs (170 g/1$\frac{1}{2}$ sticks) butter
7 ozs (200 g/scant 2 cups) icing sugar

juice of 3 oranges

non-stick crêpe pan, 8-inch (20.5 cm) diameter

First make the batter. Sieve the flour, salt and sugar into a bowl, make a well in the centre and drop in the lightly beaten eggs. With a whisk or wooden spoon, starting in the centre, mix the egg and gradually bring in the flour. Add the liquid slowly and beat until the batter is covered

79

with bubbles. (If they are to be served with sugar and lemon juice, stir in an extra tablespoon of castor sugar and the finely grated rind of half a lemon.)

Let the batter stand in a cold place for an hour or so — longer will do no harm. Just before you cook the pancakes stir in 3–4 dessertspoons of melted butter. This will make all the difference to the flavour and texture of the pancakes and will make it possible to cook them without greasing the pan each time.

Next make the orange butter. Cream the butter with the finely grated orange rind. Add the sifted icing sugar and beat until fluffy.

Make the pancakes in the usual way.

To serve: Melt a blob of the Orange Butter in the pan, add some freshly squeezed orange juice and toss the pancakes in the foaming butter; fold them in half and then in quarters (fan shapes). Serve 2 or 3 per person on warm plates. Repeat until all the pancakes and butter have been used.

Note: A tablespoon of orange liqueur e.g. Grand Marnier or orange Curaçao is very good added to the orange butter if you are feeling extravagant!

v vv *Strawberry and Rhubarb Compote

Serves 4

Rhubarb and strawberries are a wonderful combination and now that strawberries have a longer season we can enjoy them together.

> **1 lb (450 g) red rhubarb, e.g. Timperely early**
> **16 fl ozs (scant 450 ml/2 cups approx.) stock syrup (see opposite)**
> **$\frac{1}{2}$–1 lb (225–450 g) fresh strawberries — Cambridge Favourite,**
> **Elsanta *or* Rapella**

> *To serve*
> **pouring cream**
> **light biscuits**

Cut the rhubarb into 1 inch (2.5 cm) pieces. Put the cold syrup into a stainless steel saucepan, add the rhubarb, cover, bring to the boil and simmer for just 2 minutes (no longer or it will dissolve into a mush). Turn off the heat and leave the rhubarb in the covered saucepan until just cold. Hull the strawberries, slice lengthways and add to the rhubarb compote. Chill and serve with a little pouring cream and a light biscuit.

Spotted Dog

Florence Bowe's Crumpets

Pearl McGillicuddy's All-in-One Buns

Coffee Cake

Bramley Apple Jelly

Stock Syrup

Stock Syrup is the basis of homemade lemonade, fruit salad and all our compotes. We sometimes flavour it with sweet geranium, elderflower, mint or verbena leaves.

> 1 lb (450 g/2 cups) sugar
> 1 pint (600 ml/2½ cups) water

Dissolve the sugar in the water* and bring to the boil. Boil for 2 minutes, then allow to cool. Store in the fridge until needed.

* Add the flavourings at this point if using.

ᵛ Rhubarb Fool

Serves 6 approx.

> 1 lb (450 g) red rhubarb, cut into chunks
> ½ lb (225 g/generous 1 cup) sugar
> 2 tablesp. (2 American tablesp. + 2 teasp.) water
> 10 fl ozs (300 ml/1¼ cups) cream, whipped

Put the rhubarb into a stainless steel saucepan with the sugar and water, stir, cover, bring to the boil and simmer until soft, 20 minutes approx. Stir with a wooden spoon until the rhubarb dissolves into a mush. Allow to get quite cold. Fold in the softly whipped cream to taste. Serve chilled with shortbread biscuits.

ᵛ Green Gooseberry Fool

Serves 6 approx.

Tart green gooseberries picked in May make the best gooseberry fool. It will keep for several days covered in a fridge.

> 1 lb (450 g) hard green gooseberries
> stock syrup (see above)
> whipped cream

Barely cover the green gooseberries with stock syrup. Bring to the boil and cook until the fruit bursts — about 5–6 minutes. Liquidise or purée the fruit and syrup and measure. When the purée has cooled, add up to an equal volume of softly whipped cream, according to taste.

Note: A little stiffly beaten egg white may be added to lighten the fool. The fool should not be very stiff, more like the texture of softly whipped cream. If it is too stiff stir in a little milk rather than more cream.

Serve with shortbread biscuits.

ᵛ *Green Gooseberry and Elderflower Fool*
As above but add 2 elderflower heads tied in a piece of muslin to the cold syrup when adding the gooseberries, bring to the boil slowly and cook the fruit until they burst. Remove the elderflower heads before proceeding.

ᵛ ᵛᵛ *A Fresh Fruit Salad*

Serves 4

Don't fall into the trap of using too much apple. Also, it is surprisingly important to cut the fruit carefully into nicely shaped pieces, otherwise it can look a mess.

> **1 ripe pear**
> **1 ripe apple, Irish if available**
> **2 ripe oranges**
> **1 oz (30 g/generous $\frac{1}{8}$ cup) approx. castor sugar**
> **juice of 1 lemon**
> **1 ripe banana**
> **1 orange**
>
> *Optional extras*
> **1 kiwi fruit**
> **4 ozs (110 g) peeled and pipped green grapes**
> **4 ozs (110 g) fresh strawberries**
> **1 peach** *or* **nectarine**

Peel the pear and apple, cut into quarters, core and cut across the grain into slices less than $\frac{1}{4}$ inch (5 mm) thick. Peel the oranges with a stainless steel serrated knife as though you were peeling an apple, making sure to remove all the pith, then cut out each segment individually and add to the apple and pear. Sprinkle with castor sugar and lemon juice.

About 15 minutes before serving, add the sliced bananas, taste and add more lemon juice or sugar if necessary. If using kiwi fruit, grapes or strawberries add them with the orange.

Serve with a bowl of softly whipped cream.

Note: The sugar and lemon juice will draw out the juice from the fruit and give a very fresh tasting fruit salad.

^v Hazel's Bananas in Cointreau

Serves 6 approx.

This is the all-time instant pud. My sister-in-law Hazel makes it effortlessly at the table after dinner and everyone including the children love it. If you feel that Cointreau is a little excessive for a family supper, leave it out. It will still be delicious.

5 bananas
juice of $\frac{1}{2}$ lemon
juice of $\frac{1}{2}$ orange
1 generous tablesp. pure Irish honey
$2\frac{1}{2}$ tablesp. approx. Cointreau
$1\frac{1}{2}$ fl ozs (37 ml) cream

Slice the bananas into a pretty bowl, and squeeze the lemon and orange juice over the fruit. Drizzle on the honey, add the Cointreau and cream and toss well. Serve immediately.

^v Light Vanilla Ice Cream

Serves 6–8

This ice cream which is a particular favourite with children takes only a few minutes to make and is less rich than our other recipes. It's best eaten immediately or within a few days of being made. Good quality ingredients are essential here.

6 egg yolks, preferably free-range
4 ozs (110 g/scant $\frac{1}{2}$ cup) castor sugar
1 teasp. pure vanilla essence
1 pint (600 ml/$2\frac{1}{2}$ cups) good rich milk
3 fl ozs (75 ml) cream

Whisk the egg yolks in a bowl with the sugar until light and mousse like (this may take 4 or 5 minutes). Whisk in the vanilla essence, milk and cream. Strain through a fine sieve and freeze. If you have an ice cream maker, freeze according to the manufacturer's instructions, otherwise pour into a plastic box, cover tightly and pop into your freezer. Whisk once or twice as it freezes.

Sauces to serve with ice cream
All of these sauces can be made up ahead and will keep in a fridge for several days at least.

^v *Chocolate Sauce*

For the classic Poire Belle Hélène serve this chocolate sauce with poached pears and homemade vanilla ice cream.

> 2 ozs (55 g/2 squares) plain chocolate
> 1 oz (30 g/1 square) unsweetened chocolate (see glossary)
> 6 fl ozs (175 ml/$\frac{3}{4}$ cup) approx. stock syrup (see p. 81)
> rum *or* vanilla essence

Melt the chocolate in a bowl over simmering water or in a low-heat oven. Gradually stir in the syrup. Flavour with rum or vanilla essence.

^v *Butterscotch Sauce*

This irresistible sauce is delicious served with ice cream on its own, but is even better with sliced bananas.

> 4 ozs (110 g/1 stick) butter
> 6 ozs (170 g/$\frac{3}{4}$ cup) dark soft brown Barbados sugar
> 4 ozs (110 g/generous $\frac{1}{2}$ cup) granulated sugar
> 10 ozs (285 g/$\frac{3}{4}$ cup) golden syrup
> 8 fl ozs (225 ml/1 cup) cream
> $\frac{1}{4}$ teasp. vanilla essence

Put the butter, sugars and golden syrup into a heavy-bottomed saucepan and melt gently on a low heat. Simmer for about 5 minutes, remove from the heat and gradually stir in the cream and the vanilla essence. Put back on the heat and stir for 2 or 3 minutes until the sauce is absolutely smooth.

Serve hot or cold.

Note: This sauce will keep for several weeks stored in a screw-top jar in the fridge.

^{v vv} *Fresh Raspberry Sauce*

This sauce is particularly good served with homemade vanilla ice cream and sugared peaches or nectarines.

8 ozs (225 g/2 cups) raspberries
3–6 tablesp. (4–8 American tablesp.) sugar
8 tablesp. (10 American tablesp.) water
lemon juice (optional)

Make a syrup with sugar and water, cool and add to the raspberries. Liquidise and sieve, taste, and sharpen with lemon juice if necessary. Store in the fridge.

^{v vv} *Blackcurrant Sauce*
Very good served either warm or cold.

8 ozs (225 g/2 cups) blackcurrants
8 fl ozs (225 ml/1 cup) Stock Syrup (see p. 81)
4–5 fl ozs (120–150 ml) water

Pour the syrup over the blackcurrants and bring to the boil, cook for 3–5 minutes until the blackcurrants burst. Liquidise and pour through a nylon sieve. Allow to cool. Add the water.

^{v vv} *Apricot Sauce*
A few toasted flaked almonds would be delicious served with home-made vanilla ice cream and this sauce.

Whizz up the contents of a tin of apricots with some of the syrup, add the juice of a lemon, taste and add more syrup or lemon juice if needed.

^v *Almond Meringue with Strawberries and Cream*
Serves 6

We use this all-in-one meringue recipe for birthdays, anniversaries, Valentine's Day or simply for a special dessert. It's particularly delicious with strawberries, but raspberries, loganberries, peaches, nectarines or kiwi are also very good.

$1\frac{1}{2}$ ozs (45 g/$\frac{1}{4}$ cup) whole unskinned almonds
2 egg whites, preferably free-range
$4\frac{1}{2}$ ozs (125 g/1 cup approx.) icing sugar

Filling
$\frac{1}{2}$ lb (225 g) strawberries
$\frac{1}{2}$ pint (300 ml/$1\frac{1}{4}$ cups) whipped cream

Garnish
little sprigs of mint *or* **lemon balm**

Check that the bowl is dry, spotlessly clean and free from grease. Blanch and skin the almonds. Grind or chop them up. They should not be grounded to a fine powder but should be left slightly coarse and gritty (you could cheat and use nibbed almonds!).

Mark 2 x $7\frac{1}{2}$ inch (19 cm) circles on silicone paper or a prepared baking sheet. Mix the icing sugar with the egg whites and whisk until the mixture forms stiff dry peaks. *Fold* in the almonds. Divide the mixture between the two circles and spread evenly with a palette knife. Bake immediately in a cool oven, 150°C/300°F/regulo 2, for 45 minutes or until set and crisp and just brown on top. Allow to cool.

To assemble: Slice the strawberries. Sandwich the meringues together with the fruit and whipped cream, reserving a little fruit and cream for decoration. If you chill for an hour before serving it will be easier to cut. Decorate with rosettes of whipped cream stuck with little pieces of fruit. Garnish with little sprigs of mint or lemon balm.

Note: The meringue discs will keep for several weeks in a tin.

ᵛ *American Popovers*

Makes 14

This is a gem of a recipe — a variation on Yorkshire Pudding which can be made in seconds and used as a sweet pudding or just to go with a cup of tea. American Popovers are also one of our breakfast favourites, served with a blob of marmalade instead of jam and cream.

ingredients as for Yorkshire Pudding (see p. 11)

Filling
$\frac{1}{3}$ **pot homemade raspberry jam (see** *Simply Delicious 1*, **p. 76)**
$\frac{1}{4}$ **pint (150 ml) cream, whipped**
icing sugar to dust

Make the puddings and remove from the tins. Cool and fill with a blob of homemade raspberry jam and whipped cream. Dust with icing sugar and serve immediately.

Irish Farmhouse Cheeses

For me the emergence of the Irish farmhouse cheese industry has been the most exciting development on the Irish food scene in recent years. These cheeses, made by small producers all over the country, are held in the highest esteem both in Britain and on the Continent, having won top prizes in major cheese competitions. In other words, a tiny Irish industry has made an impact altogether out of proportion to its size. Many Irish farmhouse cheeses are as good as, and in some cases better than, anything produced anywhere in the world. This is fairly heady stuff, yet it comes as a surprise to most Irish people.

At Ballymaloe for the past ten years we have been proudly serving only Irish farmhouse cheeses on our cheese trolley. We find that all our guests, both local and foreign, are fascinated to taste these cheeses and hear about the charismatic people who make them (and boy, are there some characters!). Most of the cheeses are called after the townland where they are made. Each has its own particular character and the flavour changes according to the season and the pasture on which the cows, goats or sheep feed.

As farmhouse cheeses require more care than their factory counterparts, your enjoyment of them will depend on your ability to choose cheese in good condition and to look after it properly. To allow for distribution and handling, most cheeses still leave the farm underripe — some drastically so — and from there on it is a gamble. If you are lucky the wholesaler will store it carefully until it reaches the counter of one of the growing number of shops where somebody understands the importance of offering consumers cheese in prime condition. Sadly this is not always the case. A lot of good cheese is cut up into tiny pieces, some of which cannot be ripened properly no matter how much care is taken; and much of it is wrapped in the dreaded plastic film which all cheesemakers agree is detrimental to cheese.

Insist on having your cheese cut to order. If it is overripe don't buy it. If it is a little underripe bring it home, wrap it in greaseproof paper and care for it until it is in the condition you enjoy. Most Irish cheesemakers are happy to send cheese by post — a very satisfactory arrangement provided you want to buy a whole cheese. Tom and Giana Ferguson who make the wonderful Gubbeen cheese near Schull in Co. Cork have produced an excellent leaflet on caring for cheese which they will happily send anyone who provides a stamped, self-addressed envelope — and for further reading I also recommend *The Bridgestone Irish Food Guide* by John and Sally McKenna.

Vegetarians may want to use cheese made with vegetarian rennet. All major creameries and co-ops make their own vegetarian Cheddar; Cahill's Farm cheeses are made with a rennet substitute.

The following list of Irish farmhouse cheesemakers is far from comprehensive due to pressure on space. For a full list send a stamped, self-addressed envelope to CAIS — Irish Farmhouse Cheesemakers Association, 38 Molesworth Street, Dublin 2, Tel. (01) 767137.

ᵛᵛ*Ardrahan*
A semi-soft farmhouse cheese made with vegetarian rennet by Mary and Eugene Burns from the milk of their pedigree Friesian herd, in Kanturk, Co. Cork. Distinctive, rich nutty flavour and slightly crumbly texture. Tel. (029) 78099.

Cashel Blue
This exquisite blue cheese is made by Jane and Louis Grubb near Fethard, Co. Tipperary. It can be sensational when it ripens to its full maturity: sadly it is not always found like this on the cheese counter. It suffers perhaps more than any other cheese from being sold underripe when it can be chalky and salty. Many people who have not tasted Cashel Blue at its peak express surprise that this cheese is held in such high regard and wins so many prizes, but persevere — it will be worth the effort. A new Cashel White is also made. Both pasteurised and unpasteurised cheeses are made. Tel. (052) 31151.

Chetwynd
A semi-soft creamy blue cheese made by Jerry Beechinor on his farm overlooking Cork City. Rich and pungent with a close texture. Tel. (021) 543502.

Claire Coogan's Cheese
Made from unpasteurised milk on a very small scale in Castlecomer, Co. Kilkenny by Claire Coogan. Supplied by post only to selected restaurants and special clients. Well worth seeking out. Tel. (056) 41105.

Coolea
A rich and nutty Gouda type cheese with a glorious golden waxed rind made from unpasteurised milk by Dick and Helene Willems on their farm in West Cork. Tel. (026) 45204.

Cooleeney
Exceedingly good Camembert made from unpasteurised milk by Breda Maher near Moyne, Co. Tipperary. These soft cheeses are quite a challenge to handle but glorious when caught in their prime. A large Brie type is also made. Tel. (0504) 45112.

^{vv}Corleggy
Goat's milk cheese with a hard natural rind, made from vegetarian rennet by Michael and Silke Cropp on their organic farm. Tel. (049) 22219.

^{vv}Cratloe Hills
A semi-hard cheese made from pasteurised sheep's milk, in the unique shape of a Celtic cross, by Sean and Deirdre Fitzgerald near Cratloe, Co. Clare. Tel. (061) 87185.

Croghan
Like many of the other Irish farmhouse cheesemakers, Luke and Ann van Kampen from Blackwater, Co. Wexford cannot keep up with the demand for their semi-soft goat's cheese with its delicious marshy flavours and melting texture. Tel. (053) 29331.

Desmond
Hard, intensely flavoured cheese, sensational both for cooking and nibbling. *Gabriel* — very hard, with a speckled crust and mellow after-taste. These two excellent hard cheeses are made by the highly skilled cheesemaker Bill Hogan from unpasteurised milk near Schull in West Cork. Bill also makes a semi-hard Raclette cheese. All three are difficult to find in the shops but worth seeking out or ordering ahead. Tel. (028) 28593.

Durrus
A semi-hard cheese made from unpasteurised milk by Jeffa Gill at her farm in West Cork. Brine-washed with a creamy, crumbly texture when young, becoming stronger in flavour as it matures. Tel. (027) 61100.

Glen O'Sheen
One of the few unpasteurised Cheddars made in Ireland, usually matured for 4–6 months, but even better if you keep it yourself for 12–18 months. Tel. (063) 86140.

Gubbeen
Another of our top cheeses, semi-soft with a rich downy apricot-washed rind and a melting texture. This cheese is made from pasteurised milk by Giana and Tom Ferguson near Schull in West Cork. There is also an

^voak-smoked Gubbeen and some are made from vegetarian rennet. Tel. (028) 28231.

Lavistown
A moist, semi-hard cheese, reminiscent of Wensleydale, made from unpasteurised milk in Co. Kilkenny by Olivia Goodwillie; sharp pungent character and crumbly texture. Tel. (056) 65145.

Maughnaclea
If you happen to be in the Cork Market look out for cheeses made by a young French couple, Martin Guillemot and Anne-Marie Jamand, at Kealkil near Bantry, Co. Cork. They can be made from cow's or goat's milk and the type varies according to the time of year and the mood of the cheesemakers. They are invariably delicious and, despite the fact that they are made in West Cork, taste unmistakably French. Tel. (027) 66241.

Milleens
Made by the matriarch of all Irish cheesemakers, Veronica Steele and her husband Norman down on their farm on the Beara Peninsula in West Cork. A unique soft tangy cheese which changes with the seasons, held in the highest regard by cheesemakers the world over. Tel. (027) 74079.

Ring
This Gouda-type cheese made by Eileen and Tom Harty on their farm in the Gaeltacht area of Co. Waterford has a rich nutty flavour and a bright orange rind. Tel. (023) 47105.

St Killian
The biggest selling farmhouse cheese in Ireland. A hexagonal shaped downy white Camembert made from pasteurised milk by Patrick Berridge and his French cheesemaker, Alain Girod, at Carrigbyrne, Co. Wexford. Larger wheels of **St Brendan brie** are also made. Tel. (054) 40560.

St Tola
An exquisite soft goat's milk cheese made in a log shape from the milk of Meg and Derrick Gordon's spoiled goats near Inagh, Co. Clare. They also make **Lough Caum**, a hard cheese with a rich and pungent flavour which matures for six weeks, but is even better at a year old. Tel. (065) 26633.

Breads, Biscuits and Cakes

An enormous number of people love baking, and children usually start by cooking biscuits and cakes rather than savoury dishes. Nowadays, however, we are fast adopting the American food-guilt complex, so that many people won't allow themselves to make a delicious cake or some scones or even a biscuit in case they might eat them!

When I was a child there was always something in the tin in case a friend dropped in for a cup of tea or coffee, and I still perpetuate this together with the tradition of hospitality it implies. The great thing is to eat just one biscuit or slice of cake! My theory — although I'm not altogether sure it holds up — is that if it is always there you are less likely to binge. Well . . . !

If you do bake bread, I hope you will begin to seek out some of the excellent wholemeal flours produced in Ireland. Now that I have cooked abroad I realise just how good the flavour and texture of Irish flour is. When I visit friends in London I frequently bring them a present of flour, and several friends take home a sack — yes, a *sack* — of flour when they return to London after holidays, so that must say something!

Different flours suit different recipes. For Brown Yeast Bread, for example, I use Kells Stoneground Wholemeal from Co. Kilkenny which has a fine, sandy texture and a high gluten content. Howards One-way, which is stoneground in Crookstown, Co. Cork, makes delicious, nutty soda bread and comes in four textures — fine, medium, coarse and extra coarse — so you can choose the one that suits you best. Inis Glas in Co. Wexford and Ballybrado in Co. Tipperary both grind very good flour from organically grown wheat. Try as far as possible to find unbleached flour.

ᵛ*White Soda Bread and Scones

Soda bread takes only 2 or 3 minutes to make and 20–30 minutes to bake. It is certainly another of my 'great convertibles'. We have had the greatest fun experimenting with different variations and uses. It's also great with olives, sundried tomatoes or caramelised onions added, so the possibilities are endless for the hitherto humble soda bread.

1 lb (450 g/3¼ cups) white flour, preferably unbleached
1 level teasp. (½ American teasp.) salt
1 level teasp. (½ American teasp.) breadsoda
sour milk *or* buttermilk to mix — 12–15 fl ozs (350–425 ml/1½–2 scant
   cups) approx.

Firstly fully preheat your oven to 230°C/450°F/regulo 8.

Sieve the dry ingredients. Make a well in the centre. Pour most of the milk in at once. Using one hand, mix in the flour from the sides of the bowl, adding more milk if necessary. The dough should be softish, not too wet and sticky. When it all comes together, turn it out on to a floured board, knead lightly for a second, just enough to tidy it up. Pat the dough into a round about 1½ inches (2.5 cm) deep and cut a cross on it to let the fairies out! Let the cuts go over the sides of the bread to make sure of this!

Bake in the hot oven for 15 minutes, then turn down the oven to 200°C/400°F/regulo 6 for 30 minutes or until cooked. If you are in doubt, tap the bottom of the bread: if it is cooked it will sound hollow.

ᵛ*White Soda Scones

Make the dough as above but flatten it into a round 1 inch (2.5 cm) deep approx. Cut into scones. Cook for 20 minutes approx. in a hot oven (see above).

ᵛ*White Soda Bread with Herbs

Add 2 tablespoons (2 American tablesp. + 2 teasp.) of freshly chopped herbs, e.g. rosemary or sage, thyme, chives, parsley and lemon balm to the dry ingredients and continue as above. Shape into a loaf or scones and bake as for soda bread.

ᵛ*Maria Moloney's Herb and Cheese Scones

   4 ozs (110 g/1 cup) grated mature Cheddar cheese (see p. 88)
   egg wash

Make the herb dough as above. Stamp into scones, brush the top of each one with egg wash and then dip into grated Cheddar cheese. Bake as for soda scones or use to cover the top of a casserole or stew.

ᵛ*Spotted Dog

This is the traditional Irish 'sweet cake', called Spotted Dog, Curnie Cake, Spotted Dick or Railway Cake depending on the area. When I was a child it was brought out to the fields to the men during the haymaking with bottles of sweet tea wrapped in newspaper. Now we bake it for our children in the Aga every Sunday morning. Many people have forgotten it, but make it again and eat it fresh from the oven — you'll find it will bring back memories.

> 1 lb (450 g/3$\frac{1}{4}$ cups) white flour, preferably unbleached
> 1 dessertsp. sugar
> 1 level teasp. ($\frac{1}{2}$ American teasp.) salt
> 1 level teasp. ($\frac{1}{2}$ American teasp.) breadsoda, sieved
> 3–4 ozs (85–110 g) sultanas, raisins *or* currants
> 10–14 fl ozs (300–350 ml/1$\frac{1}{4}$–1$\frac{1}{2}$ cups) sour milk *or* buttermilk
> 1 egg (optional — you will not need all the milk if you use the egg)

First fully preheat your oven to 230°C/450°F/regulo 8.

Sieve the dry ingredients, add the fruit and mix well. Make a well in the centre and pour most of the milk in at once. Using one hand, mix in the flour from the sides of the bowl, adding more milk if necessary. The dough should be softish, not too wet and sticky. When it all comes together, turn it out on to a floured board, knead lightly for a few seconds, just enough to tidy it up. Pat the dough into a round about 1$\frac{1}{2}$ inches (4 cm) deep and cut a deep cross on it.

Bake in the hot oven for 15 minutes, then turn down the oven to 200°C/400°F/regulo 6, for 30 minutes or until cooked. If you are in doubt, tap the bottom: if it is cooked it will sound hollow. Serve freshly baked, cut into thick slices and smeared with butter. Simply Delicious!

ᵛ*Timmy's Deep Pan Pizza

My husband Timmy who is head chef in our house makes this deep pan pizza for the children and their friends. He often uses three or four different toppings so everyone is happy.

> 1 x White Soda Bread recipe (see p. 91)
>
> roasting tin, 14 inches (35.5 cm) x 12 inches (30.5 cm)

Firstly fully preheat your oven to 230°C/450°F/regulo 8. Make the White Soda Bread dough in the usual way. Roll it out thinly to fit the roasting tin.

Cover the dough with fillings of your choice. We sometimes use a variety, or just make a giant pizza face on a tomato fondue base with black olives for eyes and nose, anchovies for eyebrows, mouth and ear rings and lots of grated mozzarella cheese for hair.

Bake in the fully preheated oven for 25 minutes approx. Serve immediately with a good green salad (see p. 70).

Suggested toppings
1 Vegetarian — Piperonata (see p. 69), Tomato Fondue (see p. 68) or Mushroom à la Crème (see p. 16), on their own or in combination with cheese (see p. 88).
2 Piperonata (see p. 69), Irish whiskey salami, olive oil, mozzarella cheese
3 Mozzarella cheese, Tomato Fondue (see p. 68), basil oil
4 Tomato Fondue (see p. 68), anchovies, black olives, mozzarella, basil oil
5 Mushroom à la Crème (see p. 16), crispy streaky rashers, grated mozzarella cheese
6 Tomato Fondue (see p. 68), Mushroom à la Crème (see p. 16), crispy bacon
7 Piperonata (see p. 69), crispy bacon, mozzarella cheese, olive oil and so on . . .

ᵛ*Individual Soda Bread Pizzas

1 x White Soda Bread recipe (see p. 91)
fillings of your choice (see above)

Preheat the oven to 230°C/450°F/regulo 8.

Make the dough and divide it into six equal pieces; roll each one into a 6 inch (15 cm) round, $\frac{1}{4}$ inch (5 mm) thick approx. (Be careful to roll out the dough thinly or it won't cook properly on the base.) Transfer to a pizza paddle covered with gritty semolina or cornmeal, if you have one. Spread about 2 generous tablespoons of chosen topping to within $\frac{1}{2}$ inch (1 cm) of the edge. Slide the pizza off the paddle onto a fully preheated baking sheet. Cook for 8–10 minutes until crisp underneath and golden and bubbly on top.

Note: Fresh herbs may be added to the base.

ᵛ*Simply Nutritious Wholemeal Bread

Makes 1 loaf

Freshly baked brown bread is for me the basis of family food. Many people are convinced that making bread is quite beyond them, but I promise you that anyone, but anyone, could make this bread. There are several variations on this theme, all are quick and easy to make and keep perfectly for several days.

> **14 ozs (400 g/scant 3 cups) stone ground wholemeal flour — we use Howard's One-way, coarse**
> **2 ozs (55 g) white flour, preferably unbleached**
> **1 tablesp. (1 American tablesp. + 1 teasp.) bran**
> **1 tablesp. (1 American tablesp. + 1 teasp.) wheatgerm**
> **1 level teasp. ($\frac{1}{2}$ American teasp.) bread soda, sieved**
> **1 teasp. (1 American teasp.) salt**
> **1 teasp. (1 American teasp.) soft brown sugar**
> **1 egg, preferably free range**
> **2 tablesp. (2 American tablesp. + 2 teasp.) oil**
> **14 fl ozs (400 ml/scant 1$\frac{1}{2}$ cups) approx. buttermilk *or* sour milk**
>
> **loaf tin, 9 inches (23 cm) x 5 inches (12.5 cm) x 2 inches (5 cm)**

Preheat the oven to 200°C/400°F/regulo 6.

Put all the dry ingredients including the sieved bread soda into a bowl and mix well. Whisk the egg, add to it the oil and most of the buttermilk, make a well in the centre of the dry ingredients and pour in the liquid, mix well and add more buttermilk if necessary; the mixture should be soft and slightly sloppy. Pour into an oiled tin and bake for 60 minutes approx., or until the bread is nice and crusty and sounds hollow when tapped. Cool on a wire rack.

ᵛ *Banana Bread*

Makes 1 large loaf

This rich banana bread has been a great favourite of ours for years and it keeps for several weeks. Serve it thickly sliced and buttered. Black speckled bananas that one would normally consider to be overripe are perfect for this.

> **1 lb (450 g) very ripe bananas**
> **8 ozs (225 g/1$\frac{1}{2}$ generous cups) self-raising white flour, preferably unbleached**
> **$\frac{1}{2}$ level teasp. salt**
> **4 ozs (110 g/1 stick) butter**
> **6 ozs (170 g/scant 1 cup) castor sugar**
> **4 ozs (110 g/$\frac{3}{4}$ cup) sultanas *or* seedless raisins**

1 oz (30 g/¼ cup) chopped walnuts
4 ozs (110 g/½ cup) glacé cherries, washed and halved
2 eggs, preferably free-range

loaf tin, 9½ inches (24 cm) x 5½ inches (13.5 cm) x 2 inches (5 cm),
    lined with greaseproof *or* silicone paper

Preheat the oven to 180°C/350°F/regulo 4.

Sieve the flour and salt into a large mixing bowl. Rub in the butter, add the sugar, sultanas or seedless raisins, the walnuts and the glacé cherries. Mash the bananas with a fork, add the beaten eggs and mix this well into the other ingredients. It should be a nice soft consistency.

Pour the mixture into the lined tin and spread evenly. Place in the centre of a moderate oven and bake for 1½ hours. Cool before removing from the tin.

It is even nicer after a day or two.

ᵛ*Florence Bowe's Crumpets

Makes 15 approx.

Another great standby, crumpets can be made in minutes with ingredients you'd probably have to hand. My children make them and cook them directly on the cool plate of the Aga. They are also the ideal solution if you've got nothing in the tin when a friend drops in for tea, because they only take a few minutes to make. The problem is one always eats too many!

    8 ozs (225 g/1¾ cups) white flour, preferably unbleached
    2 ozs (55 g/scant ¼ cup) castor sugar
    ¼ teasp. salt
    ½ teasp. bread soda
    1 teasp. cream of tartar, e.g. Bextartar
    1 oz (30 g/¼ stick) butter
    2 eggs, preferably free-range
    8 fl ozs (250 ml/1 cup) milk

Sieve the dry ingredients into a bowl and rub in the butter. Drop the eggs into the centre, add a little of the milk and stir rapidly with a whisk, allowing the flour to drop gradually in from the sides. When half the milk is added, beat until air bubbles rise. Add the remainder of the milk and allow to stand for 1 hour if possible.*

96

Drop a good dessertspoonful into a hottish pan and cook until bubbles appear on the top. It usually takes a bit of trial and error to get the temperature right. Flip over and cook until golden on the other side. Serve immediately with butter and homemade jam or better still Apple Jelly (see p. 106).

*They are usually lighter if the batter is allowed to stand but I've often cooked them immediately with very acceptable results!

^vOatmeal Biscuits

Makes 24–32

These nutritious biscuits keep very well in a tin, and the children love to munch them with a banana. Don't compromise — make them with butter, because the flavour is immeasurably better.

1 lb (450 g/5$\frac{1}{4}$ cups) oatmeal (porridge oats)
12 ozs (340 g/3 sticks) butter
1 tablesp. (1 American tablesp. + 1 teasp.) golden syrup
1 teasp. pure vanilla essence
8 ozs (225 g/generous $\frac{1}{2}$ cup) castor sugar

swiss roll tin, 10 inches (25.5 cm) x 15 inches (38 cm)

Melt the butter, add the golden syrup and pure vanilla essence, stir in the castor sugar and oatmeal and mix well. Spread into a large swiss roll tin and bake in a moderate oven, 180°C/350°F/regulo 4, until golden and slightly caramelised — about 30 minutes. Cut into 24–32 squares while still warm.

Note: Make half the recipe if a 9-inch (23 cm) x 13-inch (33 cm) swiss roll tin is used.

Oatmeal and Banana Crunch
For an instant pudding, cover an oatmeal biscuit with slices of banana, put a tiny dollop of cream on top and eat. Simply Delicious!

Loose crumbs can be scattered over some stewed apple for an instant crumble.

^v Florrie's Chocolate and Toffee Squares

Makes 24–32

These biscuits, sometimes called Millionaires Squares, are a fiddle to make, but so many people like them that it is worth the trouble. Get the maximum flavour for your effort by making them with butter and best quality chocolate.

Pastry Base
12 ozs (340 g/2$\frac{1}{2}$ cups) self-raising white flour, preferably unbleached
4 ozs (110 g/generous $\frac{1}{2}$ cup) castor sugar
8 ozs (225 g/2 sticks) butter

Toffee Filling
8 ozs (225 g/2 sticks) butter
8 ozs (225 g/generous 1 cup) granulated sugar
4 tablesp. (5 American tablesp.) golden syrup
397 g tin Nestlé full cream sweetened condensed milk

Chocolate Top
6 ozs (170 g) Lesmé, Callebaut *or* Valrhona chocolate, melted

large swiss roll tin, 10 inches (25.5 cm) x 15 inches (38 cm)

First make the shortcake base. Mix the flour with the sugar, rub in the butter and work until the mixture comes together. Alternatively, blend the three ingredients in a food processor. Roll the mixture evenly into the lightly greased tin. Prick the base with a fork. Cook in a preheated oven, 180°C/350°F/regulo 4, for 15–20 minutes or until golden in colour and fully cooked.

Next, make the filling. Melt the butter over a low heat in a heavy bottomed saucepan. Add the sugar, golden syrup and lastly the condensed milk; stir after each addition and continue to stir over a low heat for the next 20 minutes approx. (The toffee burns very easily so don't stop stirring.)

When the toffee is golden brown, test by dropping a little blob into a bowl of cold water. A firm ball of toffee indicates a firm toffee. If it's still a little soft, continue to cook for a few more minutes but be careful — if it gets too hard it will pull your teeth out later! When it reaches the correct stage pour it evenly over the shortbread base. Allow to cool.

Melt the chocolate over a gentle heat preferably in a pyrex bowl over simmering water, or in a low-heat oven, then spread evenly over the toffee. Decorate immediately with a fork to give a wavy pattern.

Cut into small squares or fingers when the chocolate is set.

For your nearest supplier of Lesmé or Callebaut chocolate, contact Gerry Moorehead, Park House, Ratoath, Co. Meath, Tel. (01) 8256501; and for Valrhona chocolate, contact Nick Healy, SPADE, St Paul's, North King Street, Dublin 7, Tel. (01) 771026.

^v*Pearl McGillicuddy's All-in-One Buns*

Makes 24

I've never bothered to make buns by hand since Pearl gave me this recipe! It's most depressing, because even though they only take seconds to make they are actually better than the ones I used to make laboriously by hand. These buns are made by the all-in-one method in a food processor.

> 8 ozs (225 g/2 sticks) butter, chopped
> 8 ozs (225 g/scant 1 cup) castor sugar
> 10 ozs (285 g/2 cups) white flour, preferably unbleached
> 4 eggs, preferably free-range
> $\frac{1}{2}$ teasp. baking powder
> $\frac{1}{4}$ teasp. pure vanilla essence

Preheat the oven to 220°C/425°F/regulo 7.

Chop the butter into small dice (it should be reasonably soft). Put all the ingredients into the food processor and whizz for about 30 seconds. Clear the sides down with a spatula and whizz again until the consistency is nice and creamy, 30 seconds approx. Put into greased and floured bun trays or paper cases, and bake in the hot oven. Reduce the temperature to 190°C/375°F/regulo 5 as soon as they begin to rise. Bake for 20 minutes approx. in total. Cool on a wire rack and decorate as desired.

^v*Butterfly Buns*

Cut the top off the buns, cut this piece in half and keep aside. Meanwhile, put a little homemade raspberry jam and a blob of cream on to the bottom part of the bun. Replace the two little pieces, arranging them like wings. Dredge with icing sugar and serve immediately.

These buns may be iced with dark chocolate icing (see p. 100) or coffee icing (see p. 102). They are also delicious, painted with raspberry jam or redcurrant jelly and dipped in coconut.

^v*Chocolate Sandwich*

Serves 8–10 approx.

This is an old-fashioned chocolate cake, the sort that keeps in a tin for several days.

6 ozs (170 g/1$\frac{1}{2}$ sticks) butter
6 ozs (170 g/scant 1 cup) castor sugar
3 eggs, separated, preferably free-range
3 ozs (85 g/scant $\frac{3}{4}$ cup) drinking chocolate powder (not cocoa)
4 fl ozs (100 ml/$\frac{1}{2}$ cup) milk
7 ozs (200 g/1$\frac{1}{2}$ cups) white flour, preferably unbleached
$\frac{1}{2}$ teasp. baking powder

Butter Filling
1$\frac{1}{2}$ ozs (45 g/$\frac{1}{2}$ stick) butter
3 ozs (85 g/$\frac{3}{4}$ cup) icing sugar
$\frac{1}{4}$ teasp. pure vanilla essence

Chocolate Glacé Icing
2 ozs (55 g/$\frac{1}{2}$ cup) drinking chocolate powder (not cocoa)
2 tablesp. (2 American tablesp. + 2 teasp.) cold water
$\frac{1}{2}$ oz (15 g) butter
$\frac{1}{4}$ teasp. vanilla essence
8 ozs (225 g/2 cups) icing sugar
hot water

or

Dark Chocolate Icing
6 ozs (170 g/$\frac{3}{4}$ cup) icing sugar
2 ozs (55 g/$\frac{1}{2}$ cup) cocoa powder
3 ozs (85 g/$\frac{3}{4}$ stick) butter
3 fl ozs 70 ml/6 tablesp.) water
4 ozs (110 g/generous $\frac{1}{2}$ cup) castor sugar

Decoration
8 fresh walnut halves *or* chocolate coffee beans

2 x 8-inch (20.5 cm) sandwich tins

Preheat the oven to 190°C/375°F/regulo 5.

Brush the two tins with melted butter, dust with flour and line the base of each with a disc of greaseproof paper. Cream the butter, add the sugar and beat until light and fluffy, then add the egg yolks one by one and beat well between each addition. Blend the chocolate powder with the milk, add to

100

the mixture and stir well. Sieve the flour and baking powder together and stir in gently. Fold in the stiffly beaten egg whites and divide the mixture between the two prepared tins. Bake in the preheated oven for 30 minutes approx. Remove from the tin and cool on a wire tray.

Meanwhile make the butter filling. Cream the butter, add the icing sugar and beat until soft and creamy. Add the pure vanilla essence and mix again.

Next make the icing of your choice. The Chocolate Glacé Icing is lighter and less rich than the Dark Chocolate Icing (which, incidentally, is perfect for éclairs).

Chocolate Glacé Icing
Put the chocolate powder into a saucepan with the cold water, add the butter and vanilla essence and stir over a gentle heat until the chocolate is dissolved. Put the icing sugar into a bowl, add the dissolved chocolate and sufficient hot water to mix to a consistency that will coat the back of a wooden spoon. Beat until smooth and glossy.

Dark Chocolate Icing
Sieve the icing sugar and cocoa powder into a mixing bowl. Measure the butter, water and sugar into a saucepan. Set over a low heat and stir until the sugar has dissolved and the butter is melted. Bring just to the boil, then draw off the heat and pour at once into the sifted ingredients. Beat with a wooden spoon until the mixture is smooth and glossy. It will thicken as it cools.

When cold, split the cakes, spread with butter filling and sandwich together. Ice with your chosen icing and decorate with walnuts or chocolate coffee beans.

^v*Coffee Cake*

Serves 8–10

Another splendid cake which keeps well too.

- **8 ozs (225 g/2 sticks) butter**
- **8 ozs (225 g/1 cup) castor sugar**
- **4 eggs, preferably free-range**
- **8 ozs (225 g/1$\frac{3}{4}$ cups) white flour, preferably unbleached**
- **1 teasp. baking powder**
- **2 tablesp. (2 American tablesp. + 2 teasp.) coffee essence (e.g. Irel *or* Camp)**

Coffee Butter Cream (see over)
Coffee Icing (see over)

Decoration
hazelnuts *or* **chocolate coffee beans**

2 x 8-inch (20. 5 cm) sandwich tins

Preheat the oven to 180°C/350°F/regulo 4.

Line the bottom of the tins with greaseproof paper, brush the bottom and sides with melted butter and dust with flour.

Cream the butter until soft, add the castor sugar and beat until pale and light in texture. Whisk the eggs. Add to the mixture, bit by bit, beating well between each addition. Sieve the flour with the baking powder and stir gently into the cake mixture. Finally add in the coffee essence. Spoon the mixture into the prepared sandwich tins and bake for 30 minutes approx. in a moderate oven.

Cool the cakes on a wire rack. When cold, sandwich the cakes together with Coffee Butter Cream and ice the top with Coffee Glacé Icing (see below). If you would like to ice the sides also you will need to double the quantity of icing. Decorate with hazelnuts or chocolate coffee beans.

Coffee Butter Cream Filling

2 ozs (55 g/ $\frac{1}{2}$ stick) butter
4 ozs (110 g/1 cup) icing sugar, sieved
1–2 teasp. Irel coffee essence

Cream the butter with the sieved icing sugar and add the coffee essence.

Coffee Icing

8 ozs (225 g/2 cups) icing sugar
scant 1 tablesp. Irel coffee essence
2 tablesp. (2 American tablesp. + 2 teasp.) approx. boiling water

Sieve the icing sugar and put into a bowl. Add coffee essence and enough boiling water to make it the consistency of thick cream.

ᵛJulia Wight's Carrot Cake

This recipe for carrot cake is by far the best one I know and was given to me by a dear friend. It keeps for ages.

7 ozs (200 g/scant $1\frac{1}{4}$ cups) wholemeal flour
3 level teasp. mixed spice
1 level teasp. bread soda
4 ozs (110 g/generous $\frac{1}{2}$ cup) soft brown sugar
2 large eggs, preferably free-range
$\frac{1}{4}$ pint (150 ml/generous $\frac{1}{2}$ cup) sunflower oil
grated rind of 1 orange
7 ozs (200 g) grated carrot
4 ozs (110 g/generous $\frac{1}{2}$ cup) sultanas
2 ozs (55 g/scant $\frac{1}{2}$ cup) desiccated coconut
2 ozs (55 g/scant $\frac{1}{2}$ cup) walnuts, chopped

Glaze
juice of 1 small orange
1 tablesp. (1 American tablesp. + 1 teasp.) lemon juice
3 ozs (85 g/scant $\frac{1}{2}$ cup) soft brown sugar

loaf tin, 9 inches (23 cm) x 5 inches (12.5 cm) x 2 inches (5 cm), lined
    with silicone paper

Preheat the oven to 180°C/350°F/regulo 4.

Put the flour, spice and bread soda into a bowl and mix well. Whisk the eggs with the sugar and oil in another bowl until smooth. Stir in the dry ingredients, add the orange rind, grated carrot, sultanas, coconut and walnuts. Pour into the lined tin. Bake for $1\frac{3}{4}$–2 hours until well risen and firm to the touch.

Meanwhile make the glaze. While the cake is still warm prick the top with a skewer, pour the glaze over the cake and leave in the tin to cool.

Jams

There are still many people who feel that jam-making is a big performance involving masses of fruit, huge cauldrons, heaps of sugar and sticky jam jars everywhere. It doesn't have to be. The great secret is to make jam in small quantities as you need it, or when you have a little fruit left over. Fling the fruit into a wide saucepan, let it soften, add some hot sugar, quickly boil to a set and there you are! Raspberry jam takes only 8–10 minutes from start to finish. You wouldn't have found your car keys to go to the shop for a pot of jam by the time you are pouring it into the hot jars.

We make jams right through the year in small amounts. As each fruit comes into season we make a few pounds of it into jam, eat as much fresh as we can and freeze the rest. This fruit, frozen in perfect condition, makes terrific jam later on.

v vv *Seville Marmalade made with Whole Oranges*

Makes 13–15 lbs (6–7 kg) approx.

We make several marmalade recipes but this one is particularly useful because you can freeze the Seville or Malaga oranges in their short season just after Christmas and make marmalade with this recipe at any time during the year. With any marmalade it's vital that the original liquid has reduced by half or better still two-thirds before the sugar is added, otherwise it takes ages to reach a set and both the flavour and colour will be spoiled. A wide, low-sided stainless steel saucepan is best for this recipe (about 14–16 inches/35.5 x 40.5 cm wide). If you don't have one roughly that size cook the marmalade in two batches.

> $4\frac{1}{2}$ lbs (2.2 kg) Seville *or* Malaga oranges
> 9 pints (5.1 L/$22\frac{1}{2}$ cups) water
> 9 lbs (4 kg/18 cups) sugar

Wash the oranges. Put them into a stainless steel saucepan with the water. Put a plate on top to keep them under the surface of the water. Simmer very gently until soft (2 hours approx). Cool and drain, reserving the water. (If more convenient, leave overnight and continue the next day.)

Warm the sugar in a low oven. Put your chopping board on to a large baking tray with sides so that you won't lose any juice. Cut the oranges in half and scoop out the soft centre with a teaspoon. Slice the peel finely. Put the pips in a muslin bag. Put the escaped juice, sliced oranges and the muslin bag of pips into a large wide stainless steel saucepan. Bring to the boil and add the warm sugar; stir over a brisk heat until all the sugar is dissolved. Boil fast until setting point is reached. Pot in sterilised jars and cover at once. Store in a dark airy cupboard.

v vv *Strawberry Jam*

Makes 7 lbs (3.2 kg) approx.

Homemade strawberry jam can be sensational but only if the fruit is a good variety. It is one of the most difficult jams to set because strawberries are low in pectin, so don't attempt it if your fruit is not perfect. Redcurrants are well worth searching out for this jam. They are very high in pectin and their bitter-sweet taste greatly enhances the flavour.

> **4 lbs (1.8 kg) unblemished strawberries (El Santa *or* Rapella if available)**
> **$3\frac{3}{4}$–4 lbs (1.6–1.8 kg/6–8 cups) granulated sugar**
> **$\frac{1}{4}$ pint (150 ml/generous $\frac{1}{2}$ cup) redcurrant juice (see below) *or* if unavailable use the juice of 2 lemons**

First prepare the fruit juice (see below) using about 1 lb (450 g) fruit to obtain $\frac{1}{4}$ pint (150 ml) of juice. Put the strawberries into a wide stainless steel saucepan with redcurrant juice. Use a potato masher to crush about three-quarters or even more of the berries, leaving the rest intact. Bring to the boil and cook the strawberries in the juice for about 2 or 3 minutes. Warm the sugar in a low oven and add to the fruit; stir over a gentle heat until the sugar is dissolved. Increase the heat and boil for about 10–15 minutes stirring frequently.* Skim, test and pot into sterilised jars, cover and store in a cool dry cupboard.

* This jam sticks and burns very easily so be careful.

Redcurrant Juice

Put 1 lb (450 g) redcurrants (they can be fresh or frozen) into a stainless steel saucepan with 6 fl ozs (175 ml) water. Bring to the boil and simmer for about 20 minutes. Strain through a fine sieve. This juice can be frozen for use another time if necessary.

^{v vv} Mrs Mackey's Uncooked Strawberry or Raspberry Jam

This is a wonderfully fresh tasting preserve but it must be stored in the freezer or fridge.

> 1½ lbs (675 g) strawberries *or* raspberries
> 2 lbs (900 g) castor sugar
> ½ bottle Certo (*or* similar pectin-based setting agent)
> 2 teasp. lemon juice, freshly squeezed

Put the fruit in a basin or bowl, mash with the sugar and leave for 2½ hours. Stir until the sugar is dissolved, then add Certo and lemon juice, stirring for 2 minutes. Put into containers, leaving ½ inch (1 cm) when covering for expansion.

Allow to stand for 48 hours in the kitchen, seal, label and freeze. When taken out of the deep freeze, it can be kept in an ordinary fridge for further use.

^{v vv} Crab Apple or Bramley Apple Jelly

Makes 6–7 lbs (3 kg)

A great favourite, particularly irresistible on warm crumpets.

> 6 lbs (2.7 kg) crab apples *or* windfall cooking apples
> 4¼ pints (2.7 L) water
>
> 2 lemons
>
> sugar

Wash the apples and cut into quarters, do not remove either peel or core. Windfalls may be used, but make sure to cut out the bruised parts. Put the apples into a large saucepan with the water and the thinly pared rind of the lemons and cook until reduced to a pulp, approx. ½ hour.

Turn the pulp into a jelly bag* and allow to drip until all the juice has been extracted — usually overnight. Measure the juice into a preserving pan and allow 1 lb (450 g/2¼ cups) sugar to each pint (600 ml/2½ cups) of juice. Warm the sugar in a low oven.

Squeeze the lemons, strain the juice and add to the preserving pan. Bring to the boil and add the sugar. Stir over a gentle heat until the sugar is dissolved. Increase the heat and boil rapidly without stirring for about 8–10 minutes. Skim, test and pot immediately.

Flavour with sweet geranium, mint or cloves as required (see below).

* You can buy jelly bags at most kitchen shops, otherwise use a cotton pillow slip.

^{v vv} Sweet Geranium Jelly

Add 6–8 large leaves of sweet geranium while the apples are stewing and put a fresh leaf into each jar as you pot the jelly.

^{v vv} Clove Jelly

Add 3–6 cloves to the apples as they stew and put a clove in each pot. Serve on bread or scones.

^{v vv} Mint Jelly

Add 4–6 large sprigs of fresh mint to the apples while they are stewing and add 3–4 tablespoons of finely chopped fresh mint to the jelly just before it is potted. Serve with lamb.

^{v vv} Rosemary Jelly

Add 2 sprigs of rosemary to the apples as they stew and put a tiny sprig into each pot. Serve with lamb.

Store Cupboard Standbys

Potatoes

Onions

Garlic

Carrots

Pasta/noodles/macaroni

Couscous

Rice

Flour, e.g. plain, self-raising, strong brown, strong white, coarse brown

Oatmeal

Sardines and tuna fish

Sweetcorn

Tinned tomatoes

Olives

Anchovies

Eggs

Butter

Cheddar cheese

Chicken stock/cubes

Extra virgin olive oil

Ground nut and sunflower oil

Red and white wine vinegar

Good mustard

Harissa or chilli sauce

Some whole spices, e.g. coriander, cardamom, nutmeg, cumin

Good quality chocolate

Nuts, e.g. hazelnuts, walnuts, almonds

Dried fruit

Homemade jam

Honey

Marmalade

Learn to cook in Ireland at the

BALLYMALOE
COOKERY SCHOOL

The internationally acclaimed cookery school run by Darina and Tim Allen is set in the midst of orchards, organic gardens and farmland close to the sea in the lush, rolling countryside of East Cork. The formal herb garden, potager-style vegetable garden and greenhouses yield a wealth of fresh produce for a wide range of courses — some suitable for complete beginners, others aimed at experienced cooks.

All the courses reflect the Ballymaloe style of cooking, which subtly enhances the natural flavours of the best ingredients from the surrounding countryside and nearby sea. Lovely fresh eggs come from the free-range hens; meat and Irish farmhouse cheeses come from the best local producers, and fish of all kinds comes straight from the boats at Ballycotton harbour.

The informal atmosphere at the Ballymaloe Cookery School attracts students from all over the world for courses ranging from one or several days to the highly regarded 12-week professional course, which takes them from simple basic methods to advanced level.

Accommodation is available in delightful cottages in the courtyard beside the school or at Ballymaloe House.

Ballymaloe Cookery School graduates are in demand all over the world.

The wide range of courses includes Ballymaloe House specialities; Entertaining; Vegetarian Food; Seafood; Bread-making; Thai, Mexican or Mediterranean Food; Café and Delicatessen Food; Cooking for One or Two; Irresistible Breakfasts, and much more.

In recent years we have also included Gardening and Interior Design in our extensive schedule of courses.

The Shell House and expanding gardens at Ballymaloe Cookery School are open to the public from 9 a.m. to 6 p.m. daily from 1 April until the end of October.

For details write or telephone: Ballymaloe Cookery School,
Shanagarry, Co. Cork. Tel +353 21 646785. Fax +353 21 646909.